Leading with Conviction

Warren Bennis

This collection of books is devoted exclusively to new and exemplary contributions to management thought and practice. The books in this series are addressed to thoughtful leaders, executives, and managers of all organizations who are struggling with and committed to responsible change. My hope and goal is to spark new intellectual capital by sharing ideas positioned at an angle to conventional thought—in short, to publish books that disturb the present in the service of a better future.

Books in the Warren Bennis Signature Series

Leading with Conviction

Mastering the Nine Critical
Pillars of Integrated
Leadership

Shalom Saada Saar
with
Michael J. Hargrove

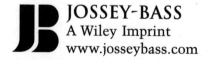
JOSSEY-BASS
A Wiley Imprint
www.josseybass.com

Published by Jossey-Bass
A Wiley Imprint
One Montgomery Street, Suite 1200, San Francisco, CA 94104-4594—
www.josseybass.com

Jossey-Bass books and products are available through most bookstores. To contact Jossey-Bass directly call our Customer Care Department within the U.S. at 800-956-7739, outside the U.S. at 317-572-3986, or fax 317-572-4002.

Wiley publishes in a variety of print and electronic formats and by print-on-demand. Some material included with standard print versions of this book may not be included in e-books or in print-on-demand. If this book refers to media such as a CD or DVD that is not included in the version you purchased, you may download this material at http:// booksupport.wiley.com. For more information about Wiley products, visit www.wiley.com.

The examples and stories in this book are based on the authors' work coaching and consulting within companies around the world. At the request of subjects and/or to protect the identities of individuals, names have been altered.

Library of Congress Cataloging-in-Publication Data has been applied for and is on file with the Library of Congress.

ISBN 978-1-118-44426-9 (cloth); ISBN 978-1-118-45910-2 (ebk);
ISBN 978-1-118-45912-6 (ebk); ISBN 978-1-118-45913-3 (ebk)

Printed in the United States of America
FIRST EDITION
HB Printing   10 9 8 7 6 5 4 3 2 1

Contents

*In memory of my parents, Rabbi Chai and
Aliza Saada, who led a tribe with love and conviction.*
—SSS
*Dedicated to my parents, Lt. Col. James and
Vivian Hargrove, who taught the lessons
of leadership through word and deed.*
—MJH

A Note from Warren Bennis

A leader has many jobs. Among them is to define reality for the rest of us, set the agenda, and get the right things done by engaging other people. It can be overwhelming. It takes years of practice, reflection, and intention, at the very least. Where does one start?

In *Leading with Conviction: Mastering the Nine Critical Pillars of Integrated Leadership,* Shalom Saada Saar starts at the place every leader must start: the self. Knowing oneself, really knowing one's own weaknesses and strengths, is a strength that is recognized widely now—however, Saar's take on this also tackles the issue of mind-set—how truly knowing oneself is the necessary first step to self-transformation. He moves on from there to describe eight other core aspects leaders must master, and this notion of the importance of mind-set stays constant.

If you are trying to become a better leader, in this book you will find a tested and inspired approach to guide you through the work that leadership requires. There are no short-cuts in this "business" of leading—however, there is wisdom and experience that can make the process that much more effective. You will find it here.

Warren Bennis

Acknowledgments

Writing a serious book about leadership is no small feat. For the last three decades we have traveled the world, meeting scores of executives in large public companies, emerging start-up organizations, and governmental agencies. In our work, we have escorted leaders on their journey—helping them to master the difficult balance between the technical tasks and the relationship aspects of leading. We have advised them to dig deeply into their character in order to understand what makes them who they truly are, and to identify the leadership legacy they aspire to leave behind.

As we pored over the data we had accumulated, we began to see the patterns that underlie good and bad leadership. More specifically, we found that certain traits influenced outcomes for individuals and organizations in critical ways. The purpose of this book is to share what we have learned about the fundamental "pillars" of leadership. Our goal is to help readers examine their beliefs and behaviors and develop the skills needed to effectively lead today's organizations with integrity and conviction.

Our deepest gratitude goes out to the many executives who invited us into their organizations and candidly shared their feelings about their fears and hopes, as well as their experiences and actions. We are indebted to them and their teams.

No book can be written without help from dedicated individuals who share the dream and devote the time and energy to transform an idea into reality. In particular, we are thankful to our talented editor, Jacqueline Murphy, who spent hours working with us and encouraging us to think succinctly and express our ideas in a simple and convincing manner. We are also indebted to Jerry Rhodes, David Workman, Charlotte Britto, Laura Bynoe, Janet Lombardo, and Lisa Wenger, who have generously provided insight and constant support throughout the process.

We are forever grateful to Warren Bennis, who has forged a path for contemporary leadership studies and served as a role model as well as a source of inspiration. We would also like to recognize Robert H. Miles and Richard Hamermesh for showing us the power of the case study method as an effective and lasting learning tool. Special thanks, also, to David Gergen and Betsy Myers, who first opened the gates at the Kennedy School of Government at Harvard University for us to explore the connection between self-knowledge and leadership.

Special thanks, as well, to Chris Caplice and Pat Hale of MIT for their support and encouragement as we wrote this book, and to the faculty and staff at Cheung Kong Graduate School of Business in Beijing and MIT.

We are particularly grateful to our research assistant, Neelima Mahajan, who sifted through a vast number of articles. She challenged our thinking with her extraordinary editorial talent.

Finally, we would like to thank our families and friends for all of the support they provided during our lengthy trips to all corners of the earth. Their devotion and encouragement were paramount in bringing this book to light. In many ways, they exercised the true meaning of leading with conviction.

Introduction

Seeing much, suffering much, and studying much, are the three pillars of learning.

—Benjamin Disraeli

Life as a leader is never easy. It is filled with obstacles, disappointments, and failures. It is also filled with victories, both large and small. Nonetheless, it is the disappointments as well as the successes that keep us coming back to try again. This, in fact, is the secret to leadership—having the conviction to return and try again. Each time we enhance our learning with more experience, better perspectives, greater effectiveness, and a thicker skin.

Having the conviction to lead is a common denominator that stretches across cultures and human history. It stems from the recognition that important events are affected by our actions. It is rooted in our acknowledgment that we have the power to shape and mold outcomes. Therein lies the purpose of this book—to get to the roots of effective leadership and offer some perspective, direction, and humble guidance on how to transform our lives and, in the process of that transformation, to improve the quality of organizations, communities, and families. It is about leading with conviction.

Leading thinkers and teachers such as Howard Gardner, Warren Bennis, Ronald Heifetz, Linda Hill, Bill George, and Daniel Goleman have contributed to the impressive body of thought leadership in this area. Their books, speeches, and classes offer compelling ideas and theories to guide leaders to become better. They stress the importance of becoming emotionally intelligent and adaptable. They point out that today's complex world requires nuanced responses and the capacity to live with ambiguity while cultivating a bias toward action. Most important, they remind us that leaders are above all human, and that conviction and self-awareness are the building blocks of effective, lasting leadership.

Our work starts where these thinkers leave off. It offers the practical and tactical tools to help you act with conviction and strengthen your capacity to lead a healthier organization. It is diagnostic and prescriptive—identifying nine pillars for lifelong learning and presenting focused strategies for developing them.

The leadership philosophy and principles that form the basis of this book are derived from years of experience working closely with executives and managers. We have conducted hundreds of coaching sessions, administered scores of 360° feedback assessments, interviewed teams, and examined various models of leadership. By no means do we claim this work to be entirely scientific, but certainly it serves as a longitudinal study representing more than three decades of working closely with multinational corporations, small startups, government agencies, and not-for-profit organizations. Through this work, we have identified several universal principles that cross time, geography, and cultural boundaries.

The leadership pillars highlighted in this book can be built, they can be taught, and they can be learned. If you choose to take on the leadership challenge, these skills are not optional. They must be deliberately and continuously practiced. Adapting to become a better leader is an endeavor with many false starts. Leadership seminars, for example, often have limited effectiveness. Although they are incisive in the moment, they are questionable in terms of having a lasting impact. You may find that you are momentarily inspired, only to become distracted again by the pressures and issues of the day—and soon you are back within your old comfort zone. There is no transformation. The change does not stick, because you haven't truly committed to the idea of change. And making a real commitment to change requires confidence in oneself—a prerequisite to leading with conviction. Leading with conviction is about an authentic passion driven by a belief and a desire to make things better.

Before we proceed with our premise—that developing nine fundamental pillars is the key to leading with conviction—

let us offer a few postulates that define the parameters of this book.

LEADING IS NOT ONLY FOR THE ELITE

First, our work focuses on *leadership with a small "l."* By this we mean that leadership is the domain of every single person. It is not a gift bestowed on only an elite few. Leadership knows no cultural, gender, or racial boundaries, and it is unrelated to any level of formal education and economic status. There are many formally educated people who find it difficult to lead themselves, let alone others. Similarly, the landscape is filled with financially privileged people who have failed at the leadership challenge.

Leadership is everywhere. It can be the supervisor who commits herself to improve the way team members work; the community organizer who wants individuals to be more aware of available health services; the pastor who desires to improve attendance of parishioners; the CEO who is fed up with the lack of customer service and commits to transforming the organization into a customer-friendly environment; the newly elected government official with hopes of meeting the expectations of his or her constituents; or parents who are committed to instilling the appropriate values in their children.

This is not a book about great leaders who appear on the world stage and single-handedly change the course of history.

Although you can learn a great deal from their experience and emulate some of their qualities, it is a formidable task to become like Nelson Mandela, who transformed his country into the Rainbow Nation; or Franklin Delano Roosevelt, who lifted a nation from its knees and restored its pride and industriousness in a time of world war and economic crisis; or Kenyan activist Wangari Maathai, who in a courageous and unique way raised the self-esteem of many downtrodden women; or the former Chinese Vice-Premier Deng Xiaoping, who, despite strong opposition, demonstrated China's strengths as an emerging nation. This is a book about everyday people finding themselves in situations where they must change the way they are running their organizations, communities, or families. This approach compels us to simplify, without trivializing, the burden and responsibility embedded in the desire to lead with conviction.

The question of whether leaders are born or made is academic. All of us, without exception, have experienced the challenges of leading others; for example, struggling to have our voice heard, gaining the respect and acceptance of our peers, negotiating with our parents for the things we want, competing with our siblings, running for an elected position in the community, searching for the right occupation, working hard to be successful, and caring for children or parents. All of these things are reminders that life offers us opportunities. As we seize them, we are actually leading, as well as gaining deeper and intrinsic satisfaction, which often results in a stronger and more meaningful sense of self.

LEADING IS A SOLITARY PURSUIT

Second, we need to *be careful with role models*. Most of us look up to some individuals whom we admire and desire to emulate. Yet the landscape is littered with leaders who have disappointed us. Like Bill Clinton, a man who could enter the history books as one of the greatest U.S. presidents ever, until he disappointed us with his conduct in his affair with Monica Lewinsky and its aftermath. Or Tiger Woods, who inspired a generation of young people who admired his sense of discipline and his accomplishments—until his fall from grace. And even the charismatic Carly Fiorina, former CEO of Hewlett-Packard, who served as a role model for many rising female leaders until late in her career at HP, when many came to believe that there was more form than substance to Fiorina's leadership accomplishments. The reality is that most role models fall short of our hopes and expectations. Frankly, they are human beings and, as such, they are fallible.

Leading with conviction is in many ways a solitary pursuit. That does not mean that you cannot learn from others, but at the end of the day your motivation has to come from your own vision and aspirations. Leadership is not a position or a role. It is an activity that slowly and gradually transforms you—and others—into something better. It takes you to a place you never thought you could reach even in your wildest dreams. The act of leading with conviction is driven by an internal desire to change lives. Furthermore, it is about expressing your own voice, realizing your vision, and conquering your fears. However, if you rely on role models, you risk losing touch with these intrinsic personal elements that give you the potential to be a leader unlike any other.

LEADING REQUIRES COURAGE

Third, *the process of transformation is never as smooth as we would like.* We all live in a society that craves instant gratification: lose weight in two weeks, smooth wrinkles in three days, have a perfect smile in three visits to the dentist, find a life partner with the click of a mouse. The process of transformation is lengthy, arduous, and, at times, painful—but it is necessary. In many ways, it is like a butterfly struggling to emerge from its cocoon. Any attempt to help the butterfly free itself can damage its wings and lead to its untimely death. We each must go through our own transformative process at our own pace, exercising our will in order to strengthen our abilities, dealing with our fears, and having the courage to break through our mental barriers.

The most intriguing aspect of the journey is the inevitability of risks and failures. Yet in the face of deep disappointment you will evolve as a leader. This is the essence of leading with conviction. In his book *The Managerial Mystique,* Abraham Zaleznik discusses the concept of a "twice-born leader."[1] It is driven by the notion that the most successful leaders are those who have met a crisis unsuccessfully. And what distinguishes them from others is their willingness to summon the courage to determine where they went wrong. Instead of blaming others, they look into the mirror and begin to understand the root causes of their own failures. Then, like the phoenix, they rise from the ashes. When the second opportunity comes, they are more seasoned, less ego-oriented and more focused on realizing their vision through the work of others. Thus they become true leaders.

LEADING REQUIRES A CERTAIN LEAP OF FAITH

Fourth, leading with conviction is, at its essence, the motivation to close gaps: to bridge the difference between the desired and the actual. The gap can be organizational, professional, or personal. Within organizations, leaders address performance and financial gaps. They mobilize resources and people in order to reach certain agreed-upon objectives. On a professional level, the gap may be between what an individual wants and what he or she has actually achieved. On a personal level, individuals might be interested in exploring the root causes of such gaps as dissatisfaction and restlessness. It takes considerable reflection to conclude "I am not satisfied at present, and I must change direction in order to bridge the gap in my life that is causing unhappiness." Although you can be helped and supported by others, you must find the courage to confront these personal gaps on your own. This is why most of us are reluctant to commit to change. Instead, we settle into comfortable, yet largely unfulfilling, routines. If leading with conviction is about transforming an organization or oneself, then each of us must find our own path to make that happen.

Yet there is no cookbook or instruction manual to follow. Instead, you must be committed to truly knowing yourself before you set out on your journey. There are some issues that you need to address as you become self-aware. The most primary is the fear factor. Confronted by change, each of us is more inclined to see the losses rather than the benefits. Such perceived losses are often the result of our defense mechanisms for dealing with ambiguity. Change means that you need to let go of the things that are familiar. Change requires new behaviors that you may not yet possess. More troubling, change seems to send a message that what you tried to do in the past was either wrong or worthless. Thus leading with conviction requires letting go of the rope while trusting that the next is within reach.

LEADING MUST BE CONSCIOUS AND PURPOSEFUL

Finally, in order to lead with conviction you cannot act randomly. We coach executives every day who are living under the microscope. From the moment they enter the workplace, all eyes are on them, examining and interpreting their demeanor. Do they greet others openly or ignore them? Do they appear approachable or distant? Do they seem upbeat or sullen? Every move sends a signal that quickly ripples out to the wider organization. People read these cues, and, based on their perception, either decide to go the extra mile—or become anxious and annoyed. For better or worse, every wrong move sends vibes to the people we lead. Thus, when we act randomly, our actions have unintended and often negative consequences. This is also true in a family setting, where the behavior of one of the spouses can trigger a chain of positive or negative behavior. For instance, often parents are not thoughtful about the behaviors they exhibit in front of their children. They may demand that their kids be respectful yet their own actions convey disrespect—a case of "Do as I say and not as I do." This is also the case for a leader who invites feedback but lets emotions guide his response to the feedback. Once you decide to embrace the leadership journey, you must be cognizant of the way you behave. Thus leading with conviction is a thoughtful and carefully crafted act of becoming.

Before we proceed to examine the leadership pillars that are the core of this book, let's take a moment to explore *why* this book will help you succeed personally and professionally.

LEADERSHIP: THE ONLY SUSTAINABLE COMPETITIVE ADVANTAGE

The work we have done and observations we have made point to several compelling reasons why allocating the time and resources required to prepare leaders to succeed is imperative. In fact, we believe that leadership is the only sustainable competitive advantage left. With products so easily commoditized and innovations promptly copied, leading with conviction is one of the very few true differentiators. The following are a few of the ways that cultivating the nine pillars presented in this book will provide an advantage and ballast for individuals and organizations.

○ *Keeping up with the pace of change.* Every generation believes they are living in a time of titanic transformation and progress, and we are no exception.[2] The challenges of our time have created new risks and potential rewards. But greater challenges require new skills. Research from the Center for Creative Leadership shows that the greater the stress an organization is facing, the more important a leader's "soft" skills become.[3] Based on a survey, researchers identified the skills—including motivation, communication, and vision—that bridge the gap when companies need to accomplish more with less. They found that "Among other things, leaders need to manage the dynamic tension between a sense of urgency and realistic patience, and between optimism and realism and openness."[4] Leading with conviction can mean the difference between a workforce that is empowered and motivated by change and one that is distracted and paralyzed by uncertainty.

○ *Winning the war for talent.* The more reliant we become on technology to manage mundane tasks, the more important it becomes to have leaders with strong pillars, committed to steering the business. People are at the center of any enterprise. And financial success alone is not enough to attract top global talent. Managing people in "generation flux"—the phrase coined by *Fast Company* to describe today's age, in which successful individuals are adaptable and can navigate uncertainty—requires a commitment to leadership development. People today see jobs as opportunities for learning and personal growth. The skills and behaviors of leaders are being tested as never before—and, given the age of instant information, the leadership scorecard is becoming ever more transparent.[5]

○ *Filling the leadership void.* Most would agree that today the typical business school curriculum is still weighted heavily on functional skills like marketing, finance, and technology. Henry Mintzberg has been making this argument for some time now, saying: "B-schools, which concentrate on the business functions, do not teach management. People learn management by focusing on their own experience and learning from their own experience."[6] Clearly, business schools, including many where we have taught over the years, have fallen short in developing the full range of skills needed to effectively lead. It's clear that supporting the needs of future leaders goes beyond finance and marketing to encompass a broader set of skills and competencies. To lead with conviction, you must be able to coach as well as you direct, listen as well as you speak, and read people as well as you can read a spreadsheet. That requires a complete range of fundamental skills, or *pillars*, as we will describe them throughout this book.

THE NINE LEADERSHIP PILLARS

The leadership pillars introduced in this book are derived from our work with a wide array of people from all walks of life: from managers working to improve their teams, to heads of families committed to providing their children with a promising future, to chief executive officers facilitating organizational transformation, to entrepreneurs aspiring to propel their ideas. Their stories, their drama, their aspirations have become the compelling motivation that has fueled our desire to create a framework of fundamentals and tools that offer leaders a practical approach to the challenges they face each day.

Each pillar—nine fundamental ideas in all—will offer advice and tools that guide you to build leadership competencies, address weaknesses, and improve your ability to lead with conviction. We use the pillars as a metaphor of support. No structure can be erected without a strong foundation, held up by an integrated series of pillars. This is the case from the ancient Greek Acropolis, to the Roman Pantheon, to modern architecture. These pillars, and the tools to build them, are the product of years of fieldwork and direct experience inside organizations large and small. They also stem from popular courses we have developed and taught at Harvard, MIT, Cheung Kong Graduate School of Business, and other leading schools in Europe. Because everyone does not have access to such courses, in this book we offer these pillars as a way to assist you in launching your journey to becoming a better leader. The pillars apply to individuals who strive to strengthen their ability to lead, as well as to organizations that endeavor to improve their chances of success by encouraging leaders at every level to become better.

Although each pillar may stand alone, their function is twofold: first, they support the overall structure; second, and more important, their support is integrated with the rest of the pillars. The integration of the pillars is the structure's source of strength and what allows it to stand the test of time. Most books on leadership focus on one or two pillars; these nine pillars together provide a more robust foundation for effective leadership.

In our view, self-knowledge serves as the central pillar; therefore all other pillars radiate from it. Throughout the ages, scholars, philosophers, and students of leadership have recognized the importance of developing the inner strength that comes from self-knowledge. The remaining pillars provide the needed structure for true and compelling leadership. When these pillars are integrated, their collective strength results in extraordinary outcomes, transforming people and organizations.

*****

The book is organized into ten chapters.

Chapter One is about building a pillar of self-awareness. Many of us find it difficult, if not impossible, to explore the roots of our own behaviors, the sources of our discontent, and the impact we have on others. Yet the path to self-discovery is crucial to anyone who aspires to lead with conviction. This pillar will enable you to get to know your own strengths and weaknesses, while increasing your aptitude in the core competencies of leadership.

Chapter Two focuses on building a pillar of balance to help you manage the conflict between tasks and people, as well as address both technical and adaptive challenges. It offers a model for learning how to maintain equilibrium between hard and soft skills, stability and change, logic and emotions, and work and personal needs.

Chapter Three describes the pillar of agility. It is about preparing you to inspire others and motivate them toward actions that result in extraordinary performance. The power of being able to work through others is more than a cliché. People truly *are* by far an organization's most valuable asset. This chapter will help you diagnose the needs in a situation, manage relationships, and prescribe the appropriate intervention.

Chapter Four examines building a pillar for leading change. Because change is the only consistent variable in life, you must learn how to anticipate it, embrace it, and successfully lead it. This is the essential role of leadership. Leading with conviction requires you to understand the dynamics of change, its impact on people, and the strategies needed to see it through.

Chapter Five focuses on the pillar for resolving conflicts. In a fast-paced world, conflicts are everywhere. When they are ignored they tend to multiply and intensify. Therefore you must understand the root causes of conflict and be skillful in addressing them. This chapter offers a roadmap for constructively resolving organizational and interpersonal conflicts.

Chapter Six addresses building a pillar of creativity. It examines your ability to synthesize analytical, empirical, and intuitive knowledge to achieve an objective. The stories and resources in this chapter are designed to help you develop an agile mind capable of avoiding complacency and embracing innovation and creativity.

Chapter Seven focuses on building a coaching pillar. It explores the dynamics of coaching and places trust at the center of the coaching process. It also presents a model that enables you to establish an honest dialogue at every level and to forge better relationships that result in greater outcomes both professionally and personally.

Chapter Eight introduces the collaboration pillar. Leading with conviction requires partners. In today's environment, no leader can realize his or her vision without the support and commitment from others. This chapter provides ideas and frameworks for forging a meaningful partnership with all stakeholders.

Chapter Nine describes the pillar that is geared toward achieving results. The ultimate goal of leadership is to reach positive outcomes. This chapter equips you with a step-by-step approach to transforming your vision into reality and to monitoring the journey to avoid unnecessary detours on the way to your desired target.

Chapter Ten, an epilogue, will help you sustain the leadership journey. Very often our resolve to lead with conviction—in business, as parents, and even just as humans—gets lost in the melee of life. Force of habit pulls us back to our old ways, and unanticipated events distract us from our journey. This chapter addresses these forces and introduces a means to overcome them.

*****

Strong and compelling leadership is the fuel that powers the organizational engine. People come to work to make a living. They also come with hopes and dreams of creating a meaningful and successful life. Leadership, then, is a profound responsibility. This explains why, when leadership is demonstrated at all levels, it creates an environment in which people are empowered to express themselves. Consequently, they feel free to unwrap the gifts of their talent to produce extraordinary results—and the latent power of leadership is unleashed when it is propelled by true conviction.

Building the pillars we describe in this book will help you develop your confidence and conviction. Lasting foundations for leadership are not built in an instant, and the most frequent cause of leadership failure is the refusal to commit. This refusal stems from our failure to see who we really are and our reluctance to hold up the mirror and take a hard look at our true selves. Therefore to lead with conviction is to know ourselves, and knowing ourselves is a fundamental obligation. In taking that obligation seriously, we open the gates to a meaningful and lasting leadership journey. This is the focus of the first chapter: the pillar of self-awareness.

1

The Pillar of Self

The greatest discovery in our generation is that human beings by changing their inner attitudes of their minds can change the outer aspects of their lives.

—William James

Wan Linyi, currently the CEO of Yang-Guang, one of the most successful land developers in China, was born in a small village in the province of Liao Ning, where he endured a childhood of extreme poverty. Yet despite many hardships—or perhaps because of them—he grew to value hard work and determination. With the support of his father, Wan Linyi recognized in his youth that the only way to live up to his full potential was by leaving the village to pursue an education. As a student at Peking University, he travelled throughout China to learn about the connection between people and the natural landscape. This experience helped him to commit himself to promoting "harmony between man and nature" in his work as a developer. Although he left his village for an urban life, Wan never forgot the importance of his journey toward self-awareness. Later, when the board at YangGuang first approached him to accept the job of CEO in 2007, he politely refused. He said, "I felt I was not ready. I needed more experience and more acceptability by the people." Because he was in tune with himself, Wan was able to realize that he needed to know more about the business before accepting the top job. When he did become CEO at the end of 2008, Wan was confident in his abilities.

Wan's ability to reflect is part of what has made him an effective leader. Even as one of the youngest CEOs in his field, he is widely respected. In addition, his deep appreciation for integrity has enabled him to foster a trusting work environment and a rapidly growing organization.

Building a pillar of self-awareness is a long-term endeavor, yet it reaps benefits for organizations and individuals alike. Some companies, like Google, have already bought into this idea. Chade-Meng Tan, a forty-one-year-old engineer and Google's 107th employee, has started a course at the search engine giant's Mountain View headquarters called Search Inside Yourself (SIY). The course—which aims to improve one's "mindfulness"—is perpetually oversubscribed. What the course is really about is learning to be self-aware.

For leaders, building a pillar of self-awareness is not optional. After all, before we can be honest with others about their development needs, we need to be honest with ourselves. This is part of what Warren Bennis and Burt Nanus called the deployment of "positive self-regard." The pair argued that this capacity allows leaders to make their strengths effective and their weaknesses irrelevant.[1]

An example of this is Sir Richard Branson, the sixty-one-year-old chairman of the Virgin Group of companies. From trying on lipstick at the launch of Virgin's line of cosmetics and riding with the *dabbawallahs* in Mumbai's crowded local trains, to carrying a burlesque performer on his back, and even dressing up as a bride, Branson has pushed the limits of extremism. Branson's public persona is that of a happy-go-lucky extrovert—someone who is not worried about how others perceive him. We could easily imagine that he grew up this way. Surprisingly, that isn't the case.

The Branson we see today is the product of hard work and self-examination. In the 1980s, Branson's role model and fellow entrepreneur Freddie Laker gave Branson a piece of sound advice that would pay dividends in the years to come. Years later, during an interview with *Strategy+Business* magazine, Branson recalled,

> Freddie Laker sat me down and said, "If you are going to take on Pan Am, TWA and British Airways, you've got to use yourself and get out there and realize that if you dress up in a captain's outfit when you launch the airline, you'll get on the front page.

If you turn up in ordinary business clothes, you'll be lucky to get a mention. Remember, the photographers have a job to do: they'll turn up to one of your events and give you one chance. If you don't give them a photograph that will get them on the front page, they won't turn up to your next event."[2]

Branson went on to say, "Before we launched the airline, I was a shy and retiring individual who couldn't make speeches and get out there. I had to train myself into becoming more of an extrovert." Branson realized that he was destined to fail as a public figure in a competitive industry if he did not make some changes in style. The shy and introverted Branson had to get to know himself well enough to admit his areas of weakness in order to succeed as the entrepreneurial face of Virgin, and he tells people, "It can be done." It is a matter of conviction.

As demonstrated by Linyi and Branson, admitting your shortcomings is not easy. Yet not all of us are fortunate enough to have a supportive father, like Linyi, or a Freddie Laker in our lives to tell us the truth, so we have to commit to a journey of getting to know ourselves better. Those who jump into a leadership role without practicing self-reflection are caught ill prepared and are blind to the impact their behaviors have on others.

Research shows that when individuals become wealthy, they often continue to feel that something is missing in their lives. Likewise, in our work we consistently see executives who confess that, despite all of their achievements and material well-being, they are still searching for something and are unable to identify what it is. That *something missing* is what psychologist Abraham Maslow called the highest level of needs—or self-actualization. Most of us are so busy managing day-to-day tasks that we consider self-reflection to be frivolous. Yet studies have found that the most successful people are those who take the time to reflect. The Chinese describe this as a person's ability to *ascend* and *walk onto the balcony.* Ronald Heifetz also describes "getting on the balcony" in his breakthrough work on adaptive leadership as a way to be reflective and remain far enough above the fray to see the key patterns. As a result of the process of reflection, a person learns, and the learning, in most cases, leads to change. That change is a milestone along the path to leading with conviction.

As simple as it may sound, getting to know yourself— literally the one person you have *known* for all of your life— is one of the hardest things you will do. Most of us are what we call "prisoners of our own self-image." Whenever we engage in introspection, it is almost always to take stock of the good things. We fail to acknowledge our mistakes and notice our flaws, let alone to do something about them. And of course, those who surround us are sometimes equally guilty of propping us up. *Financial Times* columnist Lucy Kellaway put it well: "A decade of psychobabble, coaching and 360-degree feedback has made no difference. It has not changed the most basic truth: people never speak truth to power."[3]

We saw this when we met with Jane, an executive at a West Coast business magazine, in early 2000. In 360° feedback, people reported that she was abrasive and an excessive micromanager. She was rude to peers—almost abusive at times.

Worse, she wasn't aware of the impact her behavior was having on her team. When her bosses tried to discuss the problem with her, she reacted very badly and outright refused to acknowledge her shortcomings. Her direct reports wouldn't dare to speak up directly, and her colleagues began avoiding her altogether. In the end, the organization lost when good people started quitting. Eventually, Jane, who was otherwise a diligent worker, also quit because she had isolated herself within the organization.

In our work with executives and students, we have observed over and over the gap between how we perceive ourselves and how others see us. We tend to judge ourselves based on our intentions, whereas others judge us based on our actual deeds and results. If you rationalize your shortcomings instead of addressing them, blaming your leadership inadequacies on the people around you, you create a leadership gap that can damage not only your credibility but also your actual ability to succeed.

As you develop the personal capabilities that enable you to lead with conviction, it is essential that you build a pillar of self-awareness, in the ways laid out in the "Assessing Your Ability to Reflect" exercise.

Assessing Your Ability to Reflect

To assist leaders in honing their ability to reflect and learn, we have devised a simple form that illuminates the degree of self-knowledge.

Circle the number that represents the frequency with which you practice the actions in the chart, using the following values:

1 = Not at all

2 = Sometimes

3 = Most of the time

1. Review the events of the day	1	2	3
2. Examine my behavior in key interactions	1	2	3
3. Assess my decision-making process	1	2	3
4. Audit my values and how they are demonstrated	1	2	3
5. Solicit feedback from others	1	2	3
6. Evaluate my behavior under pressure	1	2	3
7. Determine how I project myself with others	1	2	3
8. Explore my positive and negative feelings toward others	1	2	3
9. Measure my progress against personal goals	1	2	3
10. Draw lessons from my experience	1	2	3

Now add up your circled numbers.

24–30 points = Very Reflective

17–23 points = Somewhat Reflective

16 points or below = Not Reflective

THE CASE FOR SELF-AWARENESS

One of the most challenging courses we have developed is called *Know Thyself.* The course guides students through a series of tests that measure their approach to decision making, personality type, thinking preferences, leadership style, response to conflict, emotional intelligence, and affinity for teamwork. The reason these measures are relevant is simple: understanding ourselves pushes us to dig deeper and thereby become more authentic leaders. It allows us to act with conviction and with purpose, rather than reactively or in a random, inconsistent manner.

Self-knowledge is a prerequisite for effective leadership for several reasons. First, self-knowledge enables us to maintain a grasp on the values that guide our actions and inspire others to follow our lead. It anchors and informs what Bill George calls our "true north."[4] It allows us to trust our instincts and to step back, reflect, and act from a place of considered conviction. And it ensures that our actions, although adapted to each specific situation, will be consistent and ring true. If we've made the effort to understand and cultivate our natural response to crises, for example, we are better positioned to take the lead in a situation of extraordinary organizational stress. Others immediately sense and are inspired by our calm authority.

Second, understanding ourselves allows us to leverage our strengths and manage our weaknesses. When we truly know ourselves, our personal difficulties and even our failures can become assets. Meeting difficult challenges provides essential learning experiences that fuel our determination to succeed and provide a foundation for future positive outcomes.

Third, getting to know ourselves allows us to break free from unhealthy cycles. Many executives, even those who are well-educated and highly trained, suffer from a lack of self-awareness, so they tend to make the same mistakes over and over again. Certain types of situations can trigger automatic, deeply ingrained reactions. Humans are creatures of habit, so breaking away from these unhealthy patterns does not come easily. Self-awareness allows us to recognize our triggers and make agile adjustments. It helps us to break out of our comfort zones and challenge ourselves to be better.

Fourth, self-knowledge allows us to be cognizant of the impact we have on others. Being oblivious can derail our career and limit our effectiveness. If we offend rather than engage, people will back away from our vision. If our actions make others feel threatened and frustrated, they will refrain from offering their real opinion, and in time they will avoid taking risks and challenging themselves at work. In addition, how we behave as leaders sets the tone in terms of values. If we are prone to bad behavior, such as a lack of empathy, it infects the corporate culture: others will follow our negative lead. All of this weakens the bonds between us and our followers and undermines performance. A leader's failure to recognize these connections can have far-reaching consequences.

The value of building a pillar of self-awareness goes far beyond all these reasons. We know intuitively that increasing our self-awareness will be fulfilling in every aspect of our lives. Without it, the ideal of leading with conviction is impossible.

Determine Your Nonnegotiables

To help the leaders we work with understand themselves and what is important to them, we ask them to make a list of what they consider their nonnegotiables. For example, many leaders list honesty as a nonnegotiable. We go on to challenge their definition of honesty and ask them to further reflect and clarify what they mean—that is, whether they practice being absolutely honest or mostly honest, and what the term "nonnegotiable" means to them. We also challenge them to effectively communicate their nonnegotiables to the people they work with. Living up to nonnegotiables helps individuals build more effective relationships and increase their credibility. It also helps them in their ongoing journey to lead with conviction.

THE THREE FUNDAMENTAL ELEMENTS OF SELF-KNOWLEDGE

The concept of self-knowledge is not new. It is deeply embedded in Asian philosophy and Judeo-Christian thought. From the Chinese perspective, underlying the work of Sun Tzu (author of *The Art of War*) and others, self-knowledge is a function of three fundamental elements: Confucianism, Taoism, and Buddhism.

Confucianism is driven by the notion that to get to know yourself, you must learn how to relate to others, and that by building harmony with others you actualize your own being. Confucianism, similar to humanism, concerns itself with man's relationship to man. Relationships are a central theme for Confucius, and his ideas are expressed in terms of (1) the Golden Rule (do unto others as you would have them do unto you), (2) understanding the necessity of acting with propriety in society, and (3) the requirement that individuals keep their word. Trust and building trust with one another is at the core of Confucianism.

In Taoism, self-awareness becomes evident when we are in harmony with our surroundings. It is manifested by moderation and humility as well as compassion and kindness. Taoists teach us that excessive drive, inflated egos, and blind ambition can be destructive forces. Taoism also holds that respecting the environment is crucial for sustainability and happiness, "like birds using currents of air to support them as they glide rather than fight the drafts."[5] Our translation of Taoism for leaders is that we need to create and sustain environments and relationships that are founded upon respect, simplicity, and receptiveness.

Buddhism is about self-actualization. As in Maslow's hierarchy of needs, the culmination of happiness is driven more by extending ourselves to help others than by helping ourselves. This is accomplished through self-reflection and concentration. Buddhism is the process of heightening one's self-awareness. It is realized when we become aware of the changes we need to make in order to reach enlightenment.

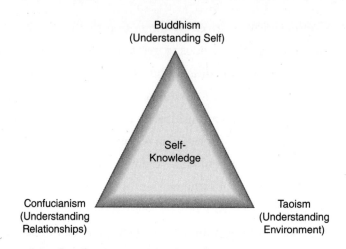

Figure 1.1: The Fundamentals of Self-Knowledge

In summary, the foundation of self-knowledge is the relationship we build with others, the harmony we must create with our surroundings, and our search for meaning and self-knowledge. Figure 1.1 depicts this in graphic form.

STRATEGIES FOR DEEPENING SELF-KNOWLEDGE

Building a pillar of self-awareness is less straightforward than we might imagine. Fortunately, there are effective techniques to help us understand and diagnose what motivates us and to identify our natural strengths and weaknesses. Some schools of thought center on holistically building on our strengths; others focus on individual skill development. Whatever the approach, the key is to recognize that, like leading with conviction, self-knowledge is a lifelong endeavor—and an essential one. We use several tools to start leaders on the journey to self-awareness.

Turning Points

One of the most effective strategies we use in helping others to know themselves involves reflecting on turning points. We begin by asking individuals to reflect on their lives and identify events and experiences that have impacted them. As they assess those experiences—positive and negative—they draw lessons about how their personalities and views in life have been shaped by those events.

For example, Doug, the CEO of a large Boston-based high-tech company, described a situation in his teens that shaped his future. Doug grew up in a small town in northern New England in a middle-class family. Overall, he was a poor student who hated school. He skipped classes on many occasions and was put on disciplinary notice. His parents were at a loss concerning what to do. Then, as a junior in high school, when Doug was seventeen, he left the class to smoke a cigarette in the washroom, thereby breaking school rules. As he lit the cigarette, his teacher burst into the lavatory stall and lifted him up by the shoulders. He looked Doug in the eye and said, "As far as I am concerned, you are worthless. There is no need for you to attend my classes from now on. I will not report this to your parents." After that, he dropped him and left.

Shaken, Doug sat in the stall for ten or fifteen minutes. This incident had such an impact on him that, right then and there, he resolved to prove the teacher wrong. It was a turning point—the beginning of his personal transformation. He worked hard, became a good student at a leading university, and years later asked the teacher to be the best man at his wedding.

Upon reflection, each of us can identify moments—more or less dramatic than Doug's—that define who we are as individuals and as leaders. Warren Bennis and Robert Thomas refer to these moments as "crucibles"—experiences so profound that they change the course of our lives. "A crucible is, by definition, a transformative experience through which an individual comes to a new or an altered sense of identity," they wrote in a *Harvard Business Review* article.[6] Understanding your own crucibles—and reflecting on how they have shaped you—provides the foundation on which to anchor your identity and lead with conviction.

Comparing Perceptions

Another way to cultivate self-awareness is to examine how we see ourselves compared to what others see. One way to do that is to use the *Johari Window,* a technique created by Joseph Luft and Harry Ingham to develop self-knowledge and improve interpersonal relationships.[7] In this particular exercise you choose five or six adjectives that describe yourself. Several col-

Table 1.1: The Johari Window

	Things I know about myself	Things I don't know about myself
Things others know about me	The public self	The blind self
Things others don't know about me	The private self	The unknown self

leagues are also asked to use adjectives to describe you. The results are then plotted on a grid that consists of four quadrants or "windowpanes," as shown in Table 1.1. Your self-description goes in the left column; the way that other people describe you goes in the right column.

The upper left quadrant—the public self—represents the part of ourselves that both we and others see. The upper right quadrant—the blind self—shows the aspects that others see but we are not aware of. The lower right quadrant—the unknown self—reveals unconscious or subconscious parts of us that neither we nor others see. The lower left quadrant—the private self—represents all that we know about ourselves but keep from others.

The Johari Window exercise, both simple and powerful, helps us understand how we reveal ourselves to others and how others perceive us. It is also an effective way to get and give feedback. In one recent instance in a training course, the Johari Window helped a woman we met, whom we'll call Jessica, identify why she was having so much trouble connecting with her team.

We were already aware that everybody in her unit—including Jessica—knew that she was extremely negative in how she interacted with others. In fact, her manager was maneuvering to transfer her, because he felt that her behavior was causing a general morale dip within her team. What the others did not know was that Jessica was struggling. Adopted as a child, Jessica had spent her life constantly grappling with feelings of resentment toward her biological mother. Being given away as a toddler had also left her with low self-esteem, which she had learned to mask in negativity. Using the Johari Window, followed by coaching, in time she was able to better understand the root cause of her behavior and consider ways to convert her negative energy into something more positive. Later, Jessica even acknowledged this personal issue to her colleagues. She followed up by publicly apologizing for her behavior. All of this went a long way toward restoring some of the lost trust between Jessica and her colleagues. It created a more harmonious relationship within her team and allowed Jessica to grow as a leader.

There is no magic bullet, but we use tools like the Johari Window to encourage leaders to consider how their perception of themselves matches how others see them.

Establishing Personality Type

A third way to become more self-aware is to identify the various characteristics of your personality and how they affect your interpersonal relationships. One common framework that can be used to shed light on your predispositions (and more specifically your personality type) is the Myers-Briggs Type Indicator (MBTI), a popular leadership development diagnostic instrument.[8] It consists of a questionnaire (which you can generally find online for free), the outcome of which enables you to gain insight into things such as whether you are outgoing or shy, whether you rely heavily on facts and details or on imagination and possibilities. This, and other tools like it, can help you to understand whether your decisions are based on principles or driven by the need for harmony. These tools shed light on whether you prefer to be organized and structured or flexible and spontaneous. The benefit is that the tools not only identify natural preferences but also suggest ways to overcome some of the shortcomings inherent in your personality. For example, if you are extremely introverted, having a better understanding of the elements of your personality might prompt you to reach out to others and become more expressive. If you are very extroverted, this might indicate that you should talk less and listen more.

Another personality preference is a propensity toward data as opposed to possibilities. This understanding can become instrumental in communicating with others. There are those who are inspired by metaphor and analysis, whereas others are more inclined toward facts and details.

Another type indicator concerns one's preference for decision making. There are those who rely on principles to arrive at conclusions, whereas others decide by their feelings. For instance, the proponents of the "three strikes" laws that mandate a life sentence without parole on a third conviction are most likely thinking types. On the other hand, "That's three strikes, but let's consider the actual magnitude of the crime and sentence more appropriately" is likely the attitude of a feeling type with a need for harmony

The last of the four Myers-Briggs indicators identifies whether a person prefers to control events by being organized and structured or is more spontaneous and prefers to go with the flow. This preference can be a source of conflict within organizational settings. For instance, organized types demand that meetings start on time and follow a formal agenda, whereas individuals who are less inclined to be structured prefer to move to the beat of their own drum and are less driven by timelines. These differing personalities are also manifested in the home, where one parent or spouse may be more structured and disciplinary whereas the other is empathic and spontaneous.

Understanding your type, and that of others around you, will help you better manage needs and relationships. It will also be extremely effective as a way to create diverse teams. Moreover, it will enhance your ability to communicate effectively to different types. However, you need to have a profound understanding of yourself before you can reach out to others. We all have certain predispositions and personality traits that drive our actions and behaviors. Understanding these traits, and how we are alike and different from others, helps us know ourselves and other people better.

3D Feedback

Finally, structured feedback (such as 360° reviews or multirater feedback) is extremely useful because it reveals how others see you, often in their own words. Feedback from direct reports, close colleagues, and senior managers enables you to discern distinctions between how individuals at various levels of the organization assess your effectiveness. Although your manager's perception may seem most important in terms of advancement and job security, it is actually your direct reports and peers who can best help you gauge how effective you are as a leader. Different programs and organizations structure 360° feedback differently, but regardless of format it is a useful way to get to know what your colleagues are thinking—especially on those things they might not vocalize without a formal performance mechanism.

Further, feedback is best achieved when a leader and his or her team have a high level of trust. Steve Wynne, the former CEO of Adidas USA, made it a common practice once a month for the leadership team members to give each other feedback on their performance and behavior, live and in front of one another. This approach, which could have been become politicized, was done in a spirit of continuous improvement. According to Wynne, it resulted in deeper relationships, better performance, and an abundance of positive energy. There were no secrets and no second guessing.

Fast 360° Feedback

Conducting a periodic leadership style questionnaire (LSQ) is a simple and effective way to help you explore the strengths and weaknesses of your leadership behavior. You can conduct your own LSQ by asking your subordinates, peers, and boss to respond to three simple questions about you. Have a colleague send the request on your behalf so that the feedback may be provided anonymously.

The three powerful questions are:

1. How would you describe my leadership style?
2. What should I do more of?
3. What should I do less of?

To paraphrase the Bard, to know or not to know oneself is a choice—and therein lies the rub. An authentic search for self, after all, requires us to hold up the mirror and to celebrate our strengths and recognize our weaknesses. The challenge, then, is to leverage our strengths and to work on our weaknesses. As so often happens in an organizational setting, there are moments or situations where weakness can become one's Achilles' heel. If you refuse to become self-aware, you will eventually hit a wall in terms of personal and career growth. As an effective leader, you must continuously challenge and change the status quo. In order to do that, you must also forge ahead by demonstrating your own willingness and capacity for self-examination, reflection, learning, and change.

One of the most important figures in Jewish history is a religious leader, Hillel the Elder. Hillel, a sage and scholar, said among other things: "If I am not for myself, who will be for me? And when I am *only* for myself, what am 'I'?"

In this famous saying, Hillel gets to the heart of self-awareness as a path to leading with conviction. You need to take the initiative for self-improvement and go through a painful process of discovery for yourself. No one can do it for you. Yet, if taken too far, you risk straying into narcissism. The second part of Hillel's idea—the notion of reaching out and building relationships and touching others' hearts—becomes paramount not only for true success but also for true self-awareness.

Searching for the truth about yourself takes courage. But actually using that self-knowledge once you possess it requires something else: an ability to balance the practical task at hand with the leadership behavior or action that will motivate the people around you. In Chapter Two, we will explore balance as the second fundamental pillar of leadership that builds a foundation for leading with conviction.

Five Guiding Principles for Building a Pillar of Self-Awareness:

1. Think about the events in your life that shaped who you are.

2. Make a habit of examining your behaviors, and asking yourself: how can I improve?

3. Know your strengths and weaknesses, and encourage feedback from others.

4. Take time to reflect and commit to constructive, meaningful action.

5. Be clear on your 360° vision for yourself—including work, community, and personal life.

2

The Pillar of Balance

People with great gifts are easy to find, but symmetrical and balanced ones never.

—Ralph Waldo Emerson

In 2001, Lawrence Summers, a brilliant economist and a consultant and advisor to President Clinton, was appointed as the twenty-seventh president of Harvard University, and a ripple of excitement spread across the campus. It was widely believed that the new president would lead Harvard from strength to strength. His vision was compelling in terms of accelerating the role of the university in the high-tech and scientific arenas. His energy was infectious. But it didn't take long for faculty and staff as well as students to erect a wall of resistance, and to defy his attempts to realize his vision.

The painful downfall of Summers at Harvard was the result of his approach in dealing with people in an institution that relied heavily on soft power. In a relatively short period of time, he alienated faculty and others. A series of internal standoffs and deteriorating relationships culminated in a high-profile incident in which Summers publicly questioned whether women were innately as capable as men of excelling in math and science.[1] His difficulty in dealing with those challenges sparked a no-confidence vote by the faculty that ultimately led to his departure. Summers's difficulty in exercising leadership balance resulted in a lost opportunity to leave a great legacy. At the core, Summers's expertise and comfort level were more on the technical side, and less on the people side.

The lesson? Driving a great vision with limited people skills can slow down and hinder implementation.

On the other side of the spectrum, some would argue that President Barack Obama is an example of someone who knows how to reach out and connect with people to inspire them for change. He uses consensus as a means for decision making. Yet during his early years in office he came up short in articulating a clear agenda that truly addressed the urgent challenges facing the deteriorating economy, especially in the areas of housing and employment. An overemphasis on people gained him friends, but he lost precious time through his lack of firmness in dealing with an uncooperative Congress—time that he could have used to accomplish important tasks. Although people attributed this setback to his lack of experience, the fact is that his over-reliance on soft skills and trusting the will of the people prevented him from mobilizing resources effectively.

Both Summers and Obama, through trial and error, have most likely learned their lessons. Obama became firmer and tougher on some issues, and Summers became more aware after his painful experience, which most likely taught him that listening to others is an invaluable strength. Still, both of these presidents depict the critical need to strike a balance between tasks and people as well as know when to command and when to delegate.

Ronald Heifetz, in his insightful work with Marty Linsky, *Leadership on the Line,* makes a distinction between technical and adaptive challenges, and describes the failures of leaders who attempt to solve adaptive challenges by relying on hard skills needed to address technical problems.[2] Our observations show that when we weigh one side more than the other we are bound to make irreversible mistakes. In fact, research shows that any strength used excessively can become a liability.

THE NEED FOR BALANCE

It is becoming clear that effective leaders need to establish a strong foundation from which to balance the conflicting forces referred to by the Chinese as yin and yang. This entails the right balance of intelligence and wisdom, hard skills and soft skills, short-term and long-term, managing stability while leading change, and exerting authority while influencing others.

This critical balance is where so many leaders fall short. When conditions require them to be strategic, they remain tactical. When they need to be focused on details, they remain abstract. When they ought to influence, they command and control. This is often the case with parenting as well. When parents need to be clear, firm, and demanding, they yield and give in to whims. On the other hand, when they need to be understanding and caring, they exert unnecessary command and control. As a result, they create a gap between their intentions and their actions—and between themselves and their children.

For the past two decades, thought leaders have stressed the importance of balancing hard and soft skills to achieve strategic business goals. Yet it was not until Peters and Waterman published *In Search of Excellence* in 1982 that organizations really began paying attention to the importance of soft power. Then, in 1995, Daniel Goleman popularized the concept of *emotional intelligence,* and his landmark book on the topic became a worldwide bestseller. When the *Harvard Business Review* published a related article by Goleman in 1998, *emotional intelligence* became a corporate buzzword. The CEO of Johnson & Johnson was so impressed by the article that he sent copies to the four hundred top executives in the company worldwide.[3] Still, as we saw in the case of Larry Summers, balancing the imperatives of task and people is not something that happens on its own. We have found in our work that for many of us hard skills, just like right-handedness, are the default.

Just as the typical business school curriculum remains weighted toward hard skills like accounting, economics, finance, technology, and marketing, so too do organizations more often reward IQ over EQ. This emphasis leaves leaders short on crucial soft skills, such as communicating, listening, empathizing, mediating, and influencing.

This remains the case even though research clearly supports the idea that soft skills are essential to success as a leader. And those skills become even more important as individuals land positions higher up in organizations. According to a study at UC Berkeley, for example, emotional intelligence is more important than IQ in predicting who will achieve success in their field.[4] A Hay/McBer study comparing outstanding managers with average managers found that 90 percent of the difference was due to soft skills.[5] And in a study of what companies were looking for when hiring new employees, 67 percent of the most desired attributes were EQ competencies.[6]

Executive education often focuses on analysis over emotion for a range of reasons, but the primary rationale is that hard skills are more teachable and measureable than soft skills. It is vastly simpler, and less subjective, to test and quantify one's grasp of finance than it is to test and quantify one's communication ability. Emotions are messy, and they defy linear thinking. "At the end of the day, it's relatively easy to teach people how to run financial models. . . . What's challenging is to lead change and to manage [people]," said Eric Hirst, associate dean for graduate programs at the McCombs School of Business at the University of Texas at Austin, in the *Wall Street Journal.*[7]

This general deficiency of institutions of higher education to prepare future leaders is one reason why some of the largest organizations have felt the need to create their own leadership development programs. From IBM and GE to Apple, Siemens, and Haier, organizations have been disappointed with the lack of people skills they observe in their new hires and middle managers. In a competitive global business landscape, where there is no room for error, more and more companies recognize that their leaders lack essential soft skills.

THE LEADERSHIP SEESAW

We use a seesaw, shown in Figure 2.1, as a metaphor to illustrate the mechanics of leadership balance. Task functions sit on one side of the seesaw, with people imperatives on the other. Although our vision is the true north that guides our behavior, self-knowledge is the base of the seesaw, supporting our ability to manage the delicate balance. The better we understand ourselves, then, the stronger our foundation and the easier it is to balance competing and often conflicting demands.

Because leadership requires that we adapt to conditions in the external environment while also keeping an eye on the

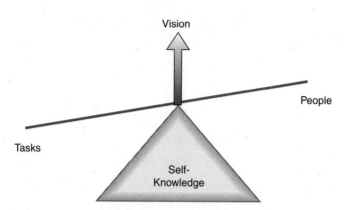

Figure 2.1: The Leadership Seesaw

vision, we are required to continuously embrace different roles. Just as being a disciplinarian is only one part of a parent's role, playing the task-focused executive is only one part of leading. In balancing multiple roles, we increase the chances that our organizations, communities, and families are maximizing their potential.

Balancing multiple roles requires the ability to deploy a spectrum of behaviors. This capability to sense and respond starts by assessing where you are on the seesaw—and knowing your default reactions and behaviors. But even as you gain a deeper understanding of yourself by identifying your natural strengths and inclinations, you need to cultivate the full blend of attributes. The best of the best can seamlessly move between the domains of logic and emotion, or between seemingly contrary ideas, in order to respond effectively to a situation. Many situations require a response that not only balances two options but also integrates them to create an ideal response.

Roger Martin, dean at the Rotman School of Management, calls this capacity *integrative thinking:* "the predisposition and the capacity to hold two [or more] diametrically opposed ideas . . . without panicking or simply settling for one alternative or another . . . in order to produce a synthesis that is superior to either opposing idea."[8]

Research on balance shows that the brain is capable of shifting between different behaviors and creating appropriate combinations, but doing so requires both reflection and dedicated practice. There is also essential learning that is derived exclusively from experience. Rising to meet everyday challenges, whether physical or mental, hones our ability to respond. If we are regularly exposed to both technical as well as people challenges, chances are we will become more comfortable with both sides of the equation. In addition, the exposure provides opportunities to calibrate the balancing act required to respond effectively to a range of situations. Still, appropriately choosing whether to use hard-power or soft-power skills in any given situation requires a great deal of mental agility. It is this intricate dance of the mind that allows us to swiftly respond to the myriad situations we encounter as leaders.

THE BALANCING ACT: TECHNICAL AND PEOPLE SKILLS

In the times in which we are living, with change and creative destruction looming around every corner, leaders need to communicate clearly and decisively. Clarity and specificity are make-or-break imperatives. Yet at the same time those that we lead need to feel trusted and inspired. After all, when we are anxious and unsure of ourselves, when we are about to fall, or when we try something new, we crave a warm word, and we look for someone to lift us up. Only then are we willing and prepared to do whatever is required.

Therefore, leaders need to choose the right tools at the right time. Overuse or underuse of skills or behaviors can affect performance and create situations that result in miscommunication and low morale. Warren Bennis famously asserted that organizations fail because they are overmanaged and underled.[9] The Leadership Checklist shows some of the skills required to manage tasks, as well as the behaviors needed to lead people and replace compliance with commitment in the process.

Leadership Checklist: A Balancing Act

To assist you in determining your tendency toward either the technical or the people side of leading, review this list and for each pair, place a check to the left of the phrase that describes your preference. If you believe that you are good at both, check both phrases. Review your results and consider your balance.

Technical	People
State the Mission	Inspire the Vision
Define Goals	Provide Direction
Be Tactical	Be Strategic
Think Linear	Think Lateral
Draft Plans	Solicit Ideas
Ensure Stability	Encourage Change
Establish Policies	Share the Values
Describe Details	Explain the Big Picture
Clarify and Define	Tolerate Ambiguity
Use Logic	Demonstrate Passion
Control and Command	Delegate and Empower
Be Focused	Be Flexible
Test Assumptions	Trust Others
Hands-on	Hands-off
Define Boundaries	Bust Boundaries
Demand Compliance	Generate Commitment
Be Aloof	Be Approachable
Use Hard Power	Use Soft Power
Engage the Mind	Touch the Heart
Demonstrate Intelligence	Show Wisdom

All of these leadership behaviors are familiar to us, but do we use them at the right times? Drafting a plan to close a plant, for example, and cutting costs by certain percentages both require technical skills. Yet a computer can manage at least some of the logistical planning for us. However, inspiring individuals to channel their fears into something positive and preparing them for change is a people challenge for which creativity, encouragement, and collegiality are more appropriate.

In our work, we've seen that less successful leaders, in both business and the public sector, find it difficult to demonstrate agility or to shift their attention from the task side to the people side of the equation. This has been the case at some large organizations over the years, where turning the ship proved to be a difficult task. Some years ago, companies like GE, IBM, Citi, and Siemens, for example, put such a strong emphasis on tasks that they lost the ability to innovate. But then CEOs like Jack Welch and Lou Gerstner came on the scene. They understood the power of unleashing the creative energy of their people, and they instilled a more balanced approach. These companies took off to higher levels of performance as a result. A lack of balance and agility also explains why some high-tech start-ups fail in their infant stages. Being entirely focused on people and innovation, their leaders lack an appreciation for structure, policies, roles, and performance reviews.

Watch the Clock

To help them achieve the right balance in their commitments to tasks and people, we ask leaders to keep a two- to four-week journal of their daily activities. When the journal is complete, we ask them to bucket the activities into categories such as "developing people," "mundane tasks," and "planning meetings." Some leaders include not only work priorities in their log but also leisure activities and family time.

Once you have completed your journal, take a moment to review how you allocate your time. You can then begin to assess whether you have found the right balance or need to take steps to make adjustments in your priorities and schedule.

Building a pillar of balance is a critical part of leading with conviction. This is the true meaning of a Golden Mean, which in philosophy means finding the desirable middle between two extremes. This entails the ability to scan the environment, the courage to recognize needs, and the dexterity required to focus on soft skills like probing, listening, praising, and encouraging, or on hard skills like controlling, demanding, and stating expectations.

Although we use *task* and *people* as the primary lenses to examine each side of the balance formula, these are other elements that leaders need to consider:

Logic and Emotion

This is a balance between objectivity and subjectivity. Objectivity is often associated with IQ. Analysis, rationality, linearity, quantitative math and sciences, and facts and details are typically associated with the left-brain realm. Subjectivity, on the other hand, is often associated with creativity, imagination, emotions, and intuition, falling into the right-brain realm.

Surgeons are typically considered to be left-brain dominant thinkers—and an analytical approach is certainly beneficial in the course of their work. However, a recent study shows that patients who perceive their physician to be empathetic actually recover from illness faster.[10] Dr. James Pepple, an anesthesiologist at Mount Sinai Hospital in Baltimore, Maryland, seems to have this figured out. His approach to patient care, well known to his surgeon colleagues, is all about balancing the technical side of medicine with the desire to calm the emotions of anxious patients. Before surgery, he is direct and clear in regard to the plans, expectations, and timeline—thereby helping the patient and his family understand the realities of the procedure. Yet he also addresses the fear and anxiety his patients feel prior to surgery. He often reaches out and holds the patient's hand as the patient is going under anesthesia. Later, Pepple takes a moment away from the O.R. to meet with family members and address their anxiety. Pepple has said that it is through experience that he learned to combine logical interactions with emotional support. It is a balance that benefits his patients and their families.

Hard Power and Soft Power

According to the work of Joseph Nye of Harvard's Kennedy School, hard power, as it pertains to leadership, means getting people to do what you want with rewards and punishments. Soft power, on the other hand, uses charisma and communication. Regardless of your personal disposition or position of power, it is optimal to have both tools at your command. An environment where hard power is overused can become oppressive and create a culture of fear. Many have argued, for example, that the United States' emphasis on hard power after the end of the Cold War created a backlash that ultimately led to the rise of radical anti-Americanism. A flat world in which geographic borders fade and mass communication is instantaneous arguably requires diplomatic skills more than military prowess. Likewise, an overreliance on soft power can lead to paralysis when it is coupled with an unproductive emphasis on consensus or chronic indecision.

Maintaining Stability and Leading Change

Whether an organization needs to focus more heavily on maintaining predictable growth or encouraging innovation will depend on where it is in the competitive landscape and in its own growth cycle. But it is easy to make the wrong choice. As we have said, some start-ups focus exclusively on innovation and experimentation, even as revenues ebb and flow. A company like Apple has succeeded because it has institutionalized creativity, whereas some of its competitors lack agility because they don't have a structure, or a culture, that encourages risk taking.

The role of the leader is to challenge what worked in the past. Yet transformation is difficult because it sends a negative signal about past performance. Whether or not the feeling is warranted, change can feel like an indictment of the past. Defense mechanisms can lead to resentment and resistance. Having a balanced approach, validating past accomplishments while encouraging openness to new approaches, enables leaders to make change happen without damaging morale.

Authority and Influence

The ultimate goal of leadership is to achieve sustained high performance through both systems and people. To get there requires a delicate balance of authority and influence. The leader must be both a commander and a coach. In the public sphere, as we saw with Larry Summers and President Obama, there are myriad examples of leaders who rely too heavily on either authority or influence.

One of the most interesting and unusual examples we've witnessed of the ideal balance between authority and influence comes from when we taught leadership at a police academy in Western Connecticut. At the time, the regional Connecticut police departments and their respective municipal boards and mayors were infamously at odds with each other. Their conflicting interests led to virtual gridlock between the mayors and the chiefs of police. The chiefs, accustomed to maintaining firm control, refused to listen to the mayors on almost anything. The mayors, who were biased in their perspective against the chiefs, would retaliate by withholding budget items that the chiefs deemed critical—the municipalities held the purse strings. This counterproductive behavior went on for years, until, finally, one chief stepped forward to create a model of ongoing dialogue with his mayor.

His approach was worlds apart from that of the chiefs before him. He treated the mayor and town council as partners. He brought them into the fold by listening to their concerns and enacting their ideas. In fact, when the town board expressed concerns about the rough demeanor of police during incidents of domestic violence, this chief came up with a very softhearted solution. When responding to domestic disturbance calls, his officers were instructed to approach with all of the usual protective equipment—but also with a big *teddy bear* in hand. And it worked. It defused many difficult situations so that the police could manage the dispute without making matters worse for children on the scene. The tactic earned him a segment on the television program *60 Minutes*.

As tough as this chief was in managing the police force and responding to crime, he was also a conciliator and team builder. As a result, the town police force was well equipped and better staffed than the others in the region.

WORK AND PERSONAL LIFE

Leading with conviction requires perspective. One way to establish a healthy perspective is by maintaining a balance between work and personal activities such as family and outside interests. One individual we know who exhibits a unique ability in the art of balance is our own colleague at the Center for Leadership Development, Charlotte Britto. A single parent of eight children and a grandmother of eighteen, Britto takes balancing work and family seriously.

For starters, she makes her own hours. Because many of her clients are in Asia, Britto schedules her time on a world clock, dividing her day into three "shifts." She begins her work day early, during the evening hours of her Asian clients. Her second shift, the family shift, begins as Asia heads to bed, in her early afternoon, as she attends family activities or sporting events with her grandchildren. This shift concludes after an early dinner with the family around the kitchen table. Finally, about 7:00 in the evening, now morning for Asia, she announces to the family, "Asia is awake" and heads off to her home office, finalizing her work day, often with conference calls scheduled at 10 or 11 PM. She also is deliberate in planning monthly dates with each of her children who live locally, weekly dates with several friends, and quarterly one-on-ones with her local grand-children. Britto is a master at balance, in part because she is incredibly efficient and prolific. But there are other reasons.

First, she is entirely transparent with clients and col-leagues about her desire to achieve a balanced life. Because of that transparency, and because she is so good at her job, Britto has managed something that most management consultants only dream of: her clients are willing to come to her. In an industry where the majority of people spend over two hundred days a year on the road, Britto has cut her travel time in half because her clients are so dedicated to the relationship. The second reason Britto has made this balance work for her is because of her commitment. A gifted trainer and coach, she channels her skills into designing and delivering exceptional training programs and forging solid relationships based on trust. As a result, her clients consider her to be an indispensible partner.

Through relationship skills and efficiency, Britto strikes a balance that works for her.

A LAST WORD ON BALANCE

We have explored some of the ways leaders need to think about balance in order to motivate people and build trust, but in reality the right balance defies prescription because it is individual and ever changing. Leading with conviction requires a fluid approach to balance. As Albert Einstein said, "Life is like riding a bicycle. To keep your balance you must keep moving." As you keep moving, in response to new opportunities and changing needs, realities shift—and so must your approach.

Balance and agility are ideals that are inextricably linked. When financial performance is deteriorating and people are unclear about their roles and responsibilities, for example, an organization must focus on left-brain functions—to state clear goals, monitor performance, and provide feedback. There are also periods in the life of an organization—when opportunities arise or challenges require a more innovative approach—that weight must be shifted to the right-brain side of the seesaw. This is when probing, listening, recognizing, and supporting will be more effective. The organization whose leaders understand the full range of leadership skills and deploy them strategically will gain powerful competitive advantage. As we will see in the next chapter, this is about not only building a pillar of balance, but also having the agility to use that balance to manage and motivate others to work on your behalf.

Five Guiding Principles for Building a Pillar of Balance:

1. Commit to a process of integrating your thoughts and emotions with your actions.
2. Balance left- and right-brain functions by focusing on tasks as well as people.
3. Develop a level of comfort in switching between thoughts and insight, analysis and intuition.
4. Focus on both the technical and the psychological (understanding people) challenges.
5. Learn how to enjoy your work while also taking time for your family and personal needs.

3

The Pillar of Agility

You manage things; you lead people.

—Grace Murray Hopper

One of the root causes of executive failure is difficulty in recognizing the need to adapt. Frequently, leaders rely on what has worked for them in the past. For instance, a frontline supervisor may have, over time, developed the skills of a commander, demanding full compliance from his or her team members. Getting quick results from a command-and-control approach may create an illusion that things get done only by exerting the skills of hard power. As people get promoted, they often believe that results can be quickly achieved only through firing off orders indiscriminately.

Although this approach may be valid in some situations, it can be detrimental in others. In most cases, it creates a wide gap between a leader and those around him or her. Effective leaders understand that regardless of the industry they are in, they are in the business of people. As such, leaders must be keenly aware of the human condition. Just as they are able to interpret and assess financial statements, marketing strategies, and software packages, they also need to develop their awareness of the needs, concerns, and hopes of the people working for them.

Sun Tzu said, "The leader must adapt to the terrain." In our experience, we've seen that most cases of executive derailment are the result of individuals being unable and/or unwilling to modify their approach to suit the situation. We call this the *absence of agility syndrome.* By agility we mean the ability to scan the human landscape and diagnose individual needs and to act accordingly. This requires leaders to take on and relinquish different roles, as they are called for. At times they need to be firm, clear, and direct. Other times they may need to be supportive, encouraging, and trusting.

This concept of agility was first introduced by Paul Hersey and Ken Blanchard in their work on *situational leadership.*[1] The Hersey-Blanchard model suggests that instead of using a single approach, successful leaders should change their practices based on the readiness of the people they're leading and the specifics of the task. According to this idea, leaders should be able to place more or less emphasis on the task, and more or less emphasis on relationships with the people they're leading, depending on what's needed to get the assignment successfully accomplished. The key is to be aware of the unique needs of the situation and capable of modulating one's approach.

By any name, the ability to tap into diverse skills to artfully solve a broad range of complex problems is a leadership competency of the first order. It is also arguably an essential expression of leading with conviction, our constellation of approaches that enable us to effectively connect with others. Agility is how leaders in organizations and families address each individual's explicit and implicit needs and expectations. Just as situations won't change to suit your leadership approach, you can't expect other people to conform in ways that will make *your* job easier while still managing to accomplish their own work. You must cultivate your capacity to adapt in order to address many different needs and shifting priorities.

Sun Tzu also wrote in the *Art of War*, "A skilled commander seeks victory from the situation and does not demand it of his subordinates." The majority of leaders today use command and control as their default because people skills are so much harder to develop. Time and performance pressures drive them to use command-and-control tactics rather than seeking input and allowing people the latitude to do their work in different ways. Leaders also default to command and control because it fits their mental mind-set of how a leader is supposed to act.

Leaders who understand and deploy a full range of skills and behaviors will consistently realize higher levels of engagement, organizational learning, and individual growth.

We often use Nelson Mandela as a case in point. When he took over as president of South Africa in 1994, he was faced with a formidable task: to unify a fractured nation in the wake of apartheid. He used rugby, a sport popular with white South Africans, to connect black and white citizens with a common goal—to see their national team win the 1995 Rugby World Cup. The Springboks, South Africa's rugby team and host of the Cup tournament that year, were considered to be weak and not even much of a contender. Besides that, black South Africans disdained rugby and viewed the Springboks—a team dominated by Afrikaaners—as a symbol of apartheid. Yet Mandela, the consummate unifier, made it his mission to inspire the Springboks to greatness and ensure that the entire nation was inspired to support them. Against the odds and with a groundswell of support, the Springboks won the cup and brought South Africa closer together in the nation's first world sporting event following the demise of apartheid.

Mandela is an exceptional leader who not only understands himself well but also has a keen insight into the psyche of others. That is a rare combination that few leaders have. He is able to use this extraordinary power to galvanize people into action and make ordinary men perform extraordinary deeds. He epitomizes the words of Mahatma Gandhi: "I suppose leadership at one time meant muscles, but today it means getting along with people."

Being in tune with people and encouraging feedback and participation is more difficult and time intensive than forcing people into compliance through coercive means. It takes sensitivity, and sometimes courage, to open the door and use people skills. Building a pillar of agility, then, is a way to engender action based on commitment as opposed to compliance. Through keen awareness of yourself and your people, and by taking each situation into account, you can deploy a combination of appropriate skills and behaviors to achieve positive outcomes.

Dr. David S. Baskin of Methodist Hospital in Houston, Texas, exemplifies the ability to take on different leadership roles. As a leading neurosurgeon, Baskin is minutely aware of the critical nature of his task. Yet he appears at ease as he moves back and forth between meeting the technical challenges of complex surgery and providing the emotional support the patient and the family need in times of crisis when they are grappling with their own mortality.

Watching him at work is fascinating. His mind pierces through the MRI with precision and certainty, determining the size, scope, and complexity of a brain tumor. As he formulates a diagnosis, relying on technology and his analytical skills, he is nonetheless in constant touch with the patient. He relentlessly explains, coaches, and teaches—and asks the patient for clarification. Throughout the conversation, he conveys the message "We are in this together, my friend, and I am going to do my utmost to get you out of this—but I also need you to believe that you will come out of it." As he moves from one approach to the other, as the individual and situation dictate, he enables the patient and the family to work with him to determine the best course of action.

In fact, he calls this process the need to attain certainty. Attaining certainty, according to Baskin, is essential for both the patient and the surgeon to achieve success in a complex and lengthy surgical procedure, during which many split-second life-and-death decisions have to be made. Baskin believes that there are many levels for which achieving certainty produces a positive outcome. Physically, the patient's immune system and stress response will be positively influenced by a steadfast vision of success. Psychologically, having certainty enables complex decision making by the patient and the family. Certainty is mandatory for the surgeon who tackles operations deemed to be challenging and at times seemingly impossible.

Dr. Baskin's ability to expertly maneuver multiple roles has been key in his success. And we credit that same agility—being able to sense and respond to individual needs—as one of the reasons Mandela's leadership is legendary.

Unfortunately, this is not always the case. For example, Richard, the founding CEO at a Massachusetts-based life sciences start-up in the late 1990s, presents a negative case study. The environment at that time was challenging for nascent companies, but this scrappy entrepreneurial organization held the patent on a technology that could have revolutionized the way physicians share information about certain diseases. The relatively small team, led by Richard, was entirely focused on growth. Richard called the shots, and his younger colleagues appreciated his direct style and passion for results. Though not quite thirty, Richard had a string of degrees and was known for his technical smarts. In addition, he invested all of his time and energy in the organization, and it flourished in its early days as a result.

In less than a decade, Richard built the company into a $300 million business. At that point, his investors determined that it was the right moment to recruit several new managers to support Richard and take the company to the next level. Although Richard approved his new management team, the transition was rough going right from the start. Richard felt that the new executives didn't respect the culture he had so deliberately created. For their part, the new managers found Richard to be difficult, abrasive, and entirely inflexible. He became increasingly isolated.

Before long, Richard went to his advisory board of investors with a plan to restructure the company and return much of the control to himself. To his surprise, they opted instead to replace him with a new CEO—one with somewhat broader managerial experience and a much wider array of people skills. Richard left the company soon after that, well compensated but angry and discouraged.

Richard succeeded at the task of growing the enterprise, but he was not up to the challenge of providing the nuanced leadership required to take the company into the future. As smart and successful as he was, the board made the right move. The company had changed dramatically over the span of nearly ten years, but Richard's leadership style had remained essentially the same. He was standing in the way of future success.

Although not all boards take such swift and decisive action, Richard's dilemma is not uncommon: even the most accomplished executives often lack leadership agility.

A FULL SET OF TOOLS

Executives often get promoted to positions in which their old tools are less effective for performing their new roles. Instead of learning new skills, they fall back on what they are most comfortable with. Consider what that means for the people in their employ. For instance, imagine that you have a leak in your kitchen sink and you call in a plumber to fix it. You watch with eager anticipation as he cracks open his toolbox. To your surprise, you see that the only item in the box is a ten-pound hammer. Would you send him home? Of course you would.

Although you can send a plumber home, you cannot do this with your boss. Yet it is not uncommon to observe executives in positions in which the approaches or skills they need most are not in their repertoire of skills. Mastering agility means having or acquiring the ability to use the right tools for that particular job.

We often use the game of golf as an analogy for leadership agility. The objective in golf is to reach the hole in a way that generates the lowest score. This is done by assessing and evaluating a myriad of variables, including wind, humidity, direction, and type of grass, as well as the bunkers and hazards that might come into play. As a result, the golfer needs to determine the type of clubs, speed, and force required as well as the appropriate angle to strike the ball.

For instance, to start the game the golfer may select the driver in order to get the maximum distance off the tee. Following the drive, the golfer may find himself in a difficult position with the ball buried in the sand. The best club for this environment would be the sand wedge. Its primary purpose is to lift the ball out of the hazard. When on the green, where the aim is to sink the ball into the cup, the golfer must rely on a delicate approach, using the putter for a soft touch. Other clubs are used in various situations, but wherever the golfer finds himself, he must demonstrate a cool composure in order to assess the situation and select the right approach. Without that demeanor, and the ability to match the tool with the situation, the game is at risk.

This is very much the case for leaders today. Like the golfer, leaders must modify their approaches in light of ever-changing circumstances. In cases where performance is declining, the leader must probe to unravel the causes. This will assist in determining the appropriate response. There will be times when the leader, like the golfer, must select a specific club, like empowerment. This requires him to trust his team by enabling them to come to their own conclusion and take the right action. There will be other times when a failure—like the ball stuck in the sand trap—offers a unique opportunity for the leader to lift the spirits of his people by instilling in them a sense of confidence and the courage to examine the failure and learn from it for the future. There will be yet other times when the right approach is exhibited through skills such as teaching, coaching, and providing honest feedback. Finally, this also means that there will be instances when the leader must take control of the situation and use a directive style, like a golfer using the driver.

Leadership agility means being in a position to shift from a direct, authoritative stance to a softer approach that is characterized by partnership, encouragement, and empowerment. As evidenced by the story of a young engineer we'll call Paul, getting a feel for a full range of leadership tools requires trial-and-error persistence.

Six months out of graduate school, Paul was given the opportunity to lead software testing for a fighter plane touted to be many times more effective than the current class of fighters. He was equipped with a support team of five individuals. Anxious to succeed, Paul devised a strict timeline for his team to follow, and he divided up the tasks equally. Everyone had a schedule to follow, with deadlines and accountability in three-day increments. Before long, however, Paul found that although three of the team members followed his instructions, two often did not, sometimes taking up to a week to finish a two-day task. Although their work was excellent, it was not delivered within the timeline that Paul had set forth.

Each time someone deviated from the plan, Paul had to create and communicate a new schedule. Eventually, as the project deadline loomed close, Paul rolled up his sleeves and took on many of the tasks himself. The project finished almost on time, but in hindsight, Paul described it as a "horrible experience" for the entire team. Looking back, he said, "My biggest mistake was treating everybody exactly the same."

Paul realized that things could have been much more efficient if he had assigned tasks based on the team's strengths and preferences rather than on his own limited perception of them. "I was overmanaging three out of five team members," he said. As a first-time manager, he did not know how to adjust his swing based on distance, as our experienced golfer does.

In Figure 3.1, the "club" *Ask* is positioned at true north as an indicator that when you are unsure of what club to use, asking is the most effective approach. By asking, you engage the other party in a meaningful dialogue. As you probe and listen closely to the replies, you can position yourself and wisely select a suitable approach. Furthermore, the act of asking sends the message that you respect the other party, thereby forging or fortifying a meaningful relationship.

LESSONS IN AGILITY

As you look at the leadership tools listed in Figure 3.1, it should quickly become clear that leaders need to be in a position to access the entire range of possible approaches. It takes practice and maturity to assume and relinquish different roles as need dictates. We'll focus a little bit on a few of the tools that not only are critical but also exemplify the entire range.

Control	——	Be hands-on, singlehandedly and unilaterally managing the situation.
Command	——	Be firm, clear, and specific on what needs to be done.
State	——	Define goals and expectations with a time table.
Explain	——	Provide a rationale for actions and events.
Coach	——	Build the skill level of desired behaviors.
Teach	——	Prepare to impart needed information to get the work done.
Ask	——	Prepare a set of questions, and listen for responses.
Involve	——	Engage others in a common dialogue.
Encourage	——	Offer support and demonstrate caring.
Inspire	——	Lift up the spirit and galvanize others around the vision and your commitment.
Delegate	——	Select low-risk activities that can be transferred with limited authority.
Empower	——	Transfer responsibility, authority, and accountability with no interaction.
Let go	——	Be completely hands-off; allow actions initiated by others with your unwavering trust.
Monitor	——	Keep your eye on the goal, remain flexible, and be prepared to change.

Figure 3.1: Selecting the Right Club

On Empowering Others

In an environment such as today's, in which many companies are lean, leaders need to trust people to take initiative. This requires a dose of empowerment. Yet although empowerment is one of the most basic tools for motivating and energizing individuals who are ready for responsibility, it can test your skills as a leader. Being so heavily focused on delivering quarterly results forces some executives to hold tight to the reins and dial down on empowerment. After all, letting go of the controls—even when that is exactly the right course of action—can feel like a high-risk, high-reward proposition. But as a leadership tool, empowerment carries benefits that far outweigh the risks.

A scene in the movie *Hoosiers* makes this point beautifully. Based on a true story, *Hoosiers* depicts a small-town Indiana high school basketball team that wins the state championship against all odds. As the team progresses and improves, the coach needs to boost their self-assurance. To demonstrate his confidence, he slowly relinquishes control, allowing them to rely solely on their skills. Eventually, during an important game, the coach provokes the referee to throw him out, thus illustrating to the assistant coach and the team that he trusts their ability to do the right thing.

Similarly, leaders in organizations need to know when to let go of the controls and allow their best people to use their skills and, as the following case illustrates, learn from their mistakes.

Christina Lopez, the general manager of a luxury retailer in Hong Kong, told us about one of her management trainees who was in the process of selling a $5,000 watch. As the transaction was being processed, there was a problem with the bank transfer from the card to the store. It seemed like one of several possible technical glitches was delaying the close. The customer, meanwhile, was getting agitated because the transaction was taking so long. In the spirit of customer service, the trainee allowed the shopper to leave with the watch, while she followed up on the bank transfer. As it turned out, the transfer did not happen—because the customer had never approved it. Knowing that she may have caused a $5,000 loss, the trainee was extremely nervous when she went to Lopez to discuss the matter. Lopez, knowing that this individual was one of her most dedicated and diligent trainees, and perhaps a talented future manager, did not lose her composure or make accusations. Instead, she asked the question: "What did you learn?" And that was the end of it.

This story of how Lopez dealt with the issue spread like wildfire through the store. By focusing on what could be learned, Lopez reinforced the organization's commitment to the customer relationship, while also emphasizing the importance of learning as opposed to assigning blame.

When you empower, you assign the authority to act. Delegation without authority is merely a more pleasant way of directing others to do exactly what you want them to do. The challenge is to communicate your goals and expectations, set the parameters, and then get out of the way. When the goal

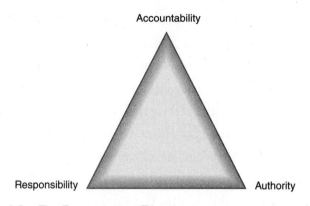

Figure 3.2: The Empowerment Triangle

is empowerment, micromanagement creates mistrust and a loss of credibility. Yet, as Lopez and her trainee demonstrated, empowerment sometimes means allowing people to make mistakes. Not only will they learn from them, but, depending on how you respond, they will also trust you more and reward the organization with higher levels of engagement and loyalty. As Figure 3.2 illustrates, *responsibility* must be associated with *authority* and *accountability for the outcome.* Likewise, responsibility without authority endangers true accountability. The three points of the Empowerment Triangle are interdependent.

Remember that empowerment does not mean disengagement; it means that you, as a leader, trust your team to do the right thing. Your role is to provide them with the resources needed to do their jobs. As you empower people, communicate your availability. Let them know they can come to you for input.

Leaders often tell us that empowerment is difficult. On further discussion, we find that the true challenge of empowerment is the fear of failure. As one executive shared, "If they fail at the assignment I delegated to them, I'm still responsible." Therein lies the challenge. As a leader, you need to be able to calculate the risk or cost of failure to the organization and the career of the person given the assignment.

Because we are often moving at a fast pace, we sometimes fail to step back and reflect on the risk in giving our associates true authority to act. Yet when delegation does not happen, people are not challenged, and learning, growth, and development are inhibited. When that happens, skills are not developed, so you, as the leader, are required to take a more hands-on approach in owning the task, which only exacerbates the problem. The better course of action is to dedicate the time and effort to reflect in order to find the courage to empower and develop your people.

On Being Supportive

Early one morning, on landing in Beijing, we saw twenty immigration officers huddled in a meeting. The manager stood off to one side of the group, listening to people's ideas about how to implement the plan of the day. She responded to a few questions, and as the meeting was coming to a close and the officers were ready to replace the night shift personnel, she walked around the circle and gave each one a pat on the shoulder. She was showing her support: it's tough work checking passports on the long day shift. When we analyze her simple act—a pat on the shoulder—we see that she was doing something uncommon. She was letting her team members know that she cares and that "we are all in this together." She understands that her role as a leader is not only to remove obstacles but also to support and inspire. Learning how to lift people's spirits and inspire them to believe in themselves is a critical element of leadership.

The dynamics in today's complex environment can cause employees to become disengaged. Therefore effective leadership requires the agility to *actively listen* to the pulse of each person and respond to his or her needs. Support and inspiration require leaders to get in touch with the needs of employees and remain in tune with the undercurrent of what people are thinking and feeling.

This heartfelt manifestation has been captured in an old Chinese parable of listening. In the third century A.D., King Ts'ao sent his son Prince T'ai to the temple to study under the great master Pan Ku so that he could be groomed as the heir to the throne. Pan Ku sent the prince to the Ming-Li Forest and asked him to return after one year and describe the sound of the forest. When the prince returned, he told Pan Ku what he had heard: he had heard birdsong, the chirping of crickets, the sound of the grass and rustle of the leaves as they were ruffled by the gentle wind, the buzzing of the bees, and the howling wind.

That wasn't good enough for Pan Ku, and he promptly sent the prince back to the forest—to do the same thing. The young prince wandered around the forest, listening to the same sounds he had listened to before. One morning, as he sat under the trees, it suddenly dawned on him. He began noticing sounds he had never heard before. He strained his ears and the sounds started becoming all the more clear. Enlightened, he went back to Pan Ku and said, "Master, when I listened most closely, I could hear the unheard—the sound of flowers opening, the sound of the sun warming the earth, and the sound of the grass drinking the morning dew." That was what Pan Ku was looking for. As he explained to the young prince, "To hear the unheard is a necessary discipline to be a good leader."[2]

Caring for people requires one to suspend judgment; to listen and then ask questions that will help others think through their position. Listen in order to understand and restate what the person has said. Disclose something from your experience, but refrain from offering your own solution. Your body language should demonstrate openness. Express your confidence in the individual's ability, and endorse their past performance. You can help by showing that you empathize with the challenges the person is facing. Above all, be sincere. The failure to be authentic will immediately and fatally undermine your effectiveness as a supportive leader.

On Being a Coach

Andy Grove of Intel once said, "Hire for attitude and train for skill." Leading with conviction requires you to carve time out of your day to play the role of the coach. But remember that coaching is teaching—it calls for openness, patience, and perseverance. It requires leaders to explain the process, the rationale, and the reasoning behind a policy or decision. In addition, teaching is most effective when people can look up to you as a role model.

Returning to the movie *Hoosiers,* there is a scene in which Coach Dale is just arriving as the new coach. He is confronted by five new recruits who want to play on the team. He knows that the team is at a point where they need to get back to basics. In this instance, he is less focused on inspiring and more on teaching the rules of engagement. Relentlessly, he guides them through the fundamentals of the game. He tells them that the game is not about "shooting" but about "passing the ball . . . it is a hot potato." He huddles with them and shares his vision of playing as a team, and he clearly describes the do's and don'ts. As he teaches, the players sense his sincerity and learn from his example. Ultimately, the coach teaches them that winning requires them to delay their own personal gratification and work as a unified team focused on a common vision.

On Taking Control

As indicated earlier, there are times when leaders must be clear about expectations. In fact, in times of crisis we want our leaders to be directive. We want them to take command and show us the way out. We are willing to submit from a place of trust that our leaders are doing the right thing. Their directive is in many ways an expression of our wishes in these circumstances.

Because control situations require direct oversight and clear communication, these are the times when you as a leader may need to level with a person or group of people. Leveling is the process of letting others know exactly where you stand and what you expect. In many cases, leveling can be an uncomfortable activity, because most leaders are reluctant to be entirely straightforward when mistakes are made. Yet with leveling, by being honest and clear you create a learning environment wherein negative feedback leads to development and growth. Commanding the situation, being firm and clear, calls for navigating difficult conversations using data and facts.

As always, start by managing yourself. Ask yourself whether you feel hostile or defensive toward the person or people you need to direct. Manage your emotional reactions and don't lose your composure. If your message is unpopular, as directives sometimes are, then people may react in ways that could throw you off. Hold back your first reaction and maintain control of the conversation.

When leveling, don't demand an immediate response. It is far more effective to give the person a day or two to think about your comments. This allows time for reflection as opposed to reaction. When you level, timing is crucial because it requires you to be calm, composed, and factual. Leveling when you are feeling overly stressed can cause you to cross the line from leveling into unloading. Although your intention is to clear the air and help the person learn, under stress your behavior may be overly emotional or even abusive.

In another scene in *Hoosiers,* Coach Dale is being challenged by a popular player who is unwilling to follow the rules. The coach asks him to leave the practice and return only when he is willing to comply. The coach understands that he is at risk of losing the rest of the players as a result, yet he sees that allowing the player to defy the rules is a greater risk. Standing up to challenges in a command situation is an acid test that every leader faces. It requires toeing the line and having the courage to express an unpopular yet necessary perspective.

This became the case when Norman Blake took over the Baltimore-based insurance provider USF&G when it was on the brink of bankruptcy in 1990. At the time, Blake recognized that some of the key officers at USF&G did not have the know-how to make the tough call to lay off employees. In the course of more than one hundred years as a southern U.S. company, USF&G had developed a culture in which difficult conversations were avoided. Blake, as a former GE executive, understood the importance of being firm and clear—commanding and controlling. He had a very clear picture of what needed to happen in order to save the company.

Blake started with a campaign to fix the foundation, in which he locked in on underwriting discipline, focusing the business, cost containment, and reducing headcount. When the business stabilized and returned to profitability, he moved to a phase of leveraging leadership. With that, he expanded into new product lines, developed people, and started the

USF&G Leadership Institute. In less than five years, under Blake's leadership, the company was saved and later sold to the St. Paul Companies.

Blake was keenly aware of his own strengths and weaknesses. In general, people considered him to be tough yet ethical, direct yet fair. This blending strengthened his role as an effective leader while leveraging the full potential of team members. Following Blake's tenure at USF&G, a number of executives who were trained under him went on to lead other companies. Although he was deemed to be a demanding command-and-control style leader, he was also widely respected during his time at USF&G for his ability to work through others in a direct and honest manner.

Blake's commanding style was critical when USF&G was in crisis mode and in the process of being rescued. However, in a less dire circumstance another approach altogether would be called for. Figure 3.3 is designed to help you explore your ability to use the various clubs or leadership approaches described in this chapter. Rate yourself on each of the approaches on a scale between 1 (hardly used) and 5 (frequently used). Then connect the dots. The results will help you to see which clubs you are most comfortable with and which ones you need to master through practice. It is also helpful to have others rate you, as well as to ask your team to use the chart to test their strengths and weaknesses.

Once you have completed the Figure 3.3 exercise, reflect on the results and answer the following questions, which are aimed at helping you become a more agile leader.

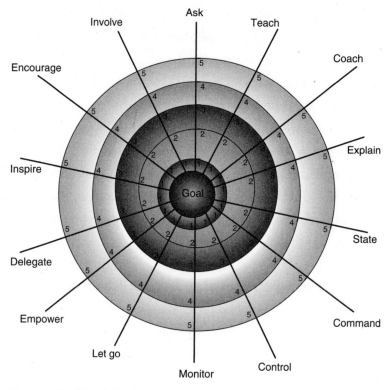

Figure 3.3: The Agility Web

1. What are the clubs/approaches you are most comfortable using?
2. What clubs/approaches are rarely used?
3. Based on your self-assessment, what clubs/approaches do you need to develop and how will you develop them?
4. List your team members and determine the best club/ approach that will increase their performance.

Thomas Jefferson said, "In matters of style, swim with the current. In matters of principle, stand like a rock." Because all organizations are dependent on the success of their people, it is critical for leaders to diagnose situations quickly and respond with the right style or approach. This means keeping an eye on the objective while remaining flexible in how you achieve it. In doing so, you must be anchored by a sense of conviction that people can improve and do better. With that conviction, leadership agility becomes more natural, because your goals and those of the organization and its people are the same.

Five Guiding Principles for Building a Pillar of Agility:

1. Scan the human landscape in terms of needs, hopes, and expectations.
2. Use the fourteen clubs to develop a wide spectrum of approaches, ranging from hands-on to hands-off.
3. When in doubt, ask and listen. This will help you understand the needs of others and strengthen the trust between you.
4. Become vigilant in interpreting the verbal and nonverbal messages that you are receiving and sending.
5. Remain focused on the goals of the organization, and help prepare others to achieve them.

4

The Pillar of Change

The world as we have created it is a process of our thinking. It cannot be changed without changing our thinking.

—Albert Einstein

Geneeral Re Corporation (known as Gen Re) is a Stamford, Connecticut–based holding company for life and property-and-casualty reinsurance, as well as risk-management services. A subsidiary of Warren Buffet's Berkshire Hathaway, Gen Re has about fifty offices around the world. Ronald E. Ferguson, in his mostly distinguished thirty-three-year career at Gen Re, served in a number of senior capacities, including president and chief operating officer (COO), before being named CEO in 1987.

He served as CEO until late 2001 and retired as chairman in June 2002. At the time Ferguson became CEO, Gen Re was considered the lone U.S. member among the troika of giants that dominated global property-and-casualty reinsurance. It was an elite, old-line company, the largest of all American reinsurers, and long viewed as one of the best managed. In his 1998 "Chairman's Letter," Warren Buffett praised Gen Re's management, concluding "There's a lot they can teach us," and he paid $22 billion on December 21, 1998, for its acquisition and for 82 percent of the oldest reinsurance company in the world, Cologne Re.[1]

When Gen Re took over Cologne Re, Ferguson faced a formidable challenge. The differences between the two companies were immense. On the one side, Cologne Re was known for its international presence in more than fifteen countries. Its business relied on relationships, and it was heavily marketing focused. On the other side, Gen Re was a more traditional American reinsurance company that had built its reputation solidly on strict underwriting standards. It was far less focused on relationships. With differing values and opposing cultures, the merger created serious problems for both organizations. The clash between the two companies caused senior leadership at Gen Re to become distracted from the actual day-to-day business. As a result, the employees from both organizations were more focused on the politics of the acquisition than on working together to address serious strategic and operational challenges. Thus, suspicion and mistrust developed, causing poor decisions and extensive financial losses.

Compare Gen Re during its time of change and transition with the experience of the Hong Kong–based DFS Group, a subsidiary of Louis Vuitton/Moet Hennessy (LVMH), under the leadership of Michael Schriver. The results stand in stark contrast.

In 2007, Schriver was president of merchandising at DFS, and he and the other senior leaders were scratching their heads over how to steer the organization through a major change initiative. It was a staggering task—transforming the fifty-year-old company from a successful airport discount store into a luxury retailer after the Asian economic crisis changed the landscape of their business in Japan and elsewhere. With six thousand employees in fifteen countries, DFS had their work cut out for them. But it was Schriver who stepped up to lead the charge.

After completing stints at Macy's department store, Schriver had come to DFS in 1998 to manage merchandising in their Hawaiian operation, and he later assumed the role of president of worldwide operations in 2008, when the existing president left to become CEO of the specialty retailer Dean & DeLuca. Schriver was elevated to the post in large part because his vision was what was driving DFS after years of only marginally successful change attempts.

Launched in the 1950s by founding partners Charles Feeney and Robert Miller, the original DFS organization sold cars and liquor to American servicemen returning home from Europe. The business expanded rapidly to embrace other airport duty-free concessions such as candy, tobacco, and souvenirs. By the late 1960s, business was booming thanks to brisk sales in tourist destinations in Asia. More recently, DFS launched downtown "gallerias" in locations such as Singapore, Hong Kong, and Australia. The successful galleria concept attracted the attention of LVMH in 1996, about the time one of the owners, Chuck Feeney, was ready to sell, and DFS became a part of the LVMH's portfolio of luxury brands. However, the process of changing DFS's primary equation from low-cost retailer to luxury boutique proved to be full of starts and stops. It was slow going until Schriver realized that he needed to foment a revolution.

With that revolution in mind, he worked relentlessly on communicating his vision to the key players. He scheduled numerous strategic retreats to lay out the landscape and ensure that the vision reached every part of the organization. Together with his team, Schriver launched a road show to communicate the meaning of DFS's transformation from a discount retailer to a "company of exceptional people delivering exceptional products." He even changed the recruitment process to ensure that the people selected had the right personality and profile to meet the challenges of the new organization.

Leadership development programs as well as sales associates' skill-enhancement training were designed and delivered. Throughout the DFS universe, a senior executive would attend each training program and communicate with the participants about the lessons learned. A communication process was established to open up the channels of dialogue through which the shared vision was discussed, key performance indicators were shared, and success stories were celebrated throughout the company.

It is no wonder that 2011 was the best sales year in the retailer's history and they achieved their highest-ever conversion rates and spend-per-customer. By all accounts, Schriver, who launched a systematic approach to change, was instrumental in making this success happen. In fact, in 2012 DFS set an industry precedent by winning all three core category concessions at Hong Kong International Airport and exclusive duty-free concessions at Los Angeles International Airport in the same month, competing against numerous contestants.

The examples of Gen Re and DFS teach us some critical lessons about change:

1. It is an inevitable element of organizational evolution.
2. It cannot be left unmanaged.
3. It must be spearheaded by senior leadership and embraced throughout the organization.
4. It needs to be considered not only from an operations vantage point but also from a cultural perspective.
5. Most important, a leader's tone and behavior during times of change send a message to the wider organization; people will take their cue from that and respond positively or negatively.

The wide array of change models one can choose from offer ample evidence that change is a timeless and ubiquitous challenge. For example, Harvard Business School professor and author John Kotter, a premier authority on leading change, created the well-known eight-step change process that has been applied in organizations around the world. It begins with creating a sense of urgency and ends with changing corporate culture. Before Kotter, psychologist Kurt Lewin identified the three stages of change that are still the basis of many approaches today: unfreeze, transition, refreeze. Lewin—who is known as the founder of social psychology—focuses squarely on human aspects of change. Yet another model, Otto Scharmer's "Theory U," is designed to help people break free from unproductive patterns of behavior by opening their minds to their blind spots.

At its core, leadership is about enabling and driving change: changing minds and behaviors, guiding others to change, and turning people's focus to the sweeping tide of change. Often the job of the leader is to adjust the direction of an entire organization. You may be charged with managing a change initiative that impacts a small team of colleagues or one that involves a company of tens of thousands of people. Regardless, leading with conviction requires a steady head in the face of constant and disruptive change.

THE STAGES OF CHANGE

Change is a highly emotional process. It causes a shock to our system and leads to unsettling feelings. Succeeding at change requires leaders to be open, vulnerable, and receptive to feedback, and it is most effective when we embrace it with curiosity and a willingness to learn and explore. Change is difficult in part because it often signals that something has "gone wrong," and we suspect that this may be our fault. What's more, change goes hand in hand with loss. It requires that we let go of something. In addition, change is extreme. Think back to the five or six major events in your life that have shaped you as a person. They might include the death of a parent, the loss of a job, a change in marital status, and/or the birth of a child. All of these major life events involved a transition.

Whether perceived as a positive or negative, change can be a roller-coaster ride. And, like a roller-coaster ride, change is not a straightforward process; it happens on a curve.

Elisabeth Kübler-Ross addressed the enormous change presented by dying and death with her model of five classic stages of grief: *denial, anger, bargaining, depression,* and *acceptance*. Although Kübler-Ross named the stages in 1969 to characterize the process of response to a terminal illness, the model is used today in a wide variety of clinical and organizational settings working with organizations undergoing major changes. In our work with organizations, we use a four-stage model of transition, also created by Kübler-Ross: *denial, resistance, exploration,* and *acceptance* (see Table 4.1). All of us have experienced these stages, both personally and professionally, and it is important for leaders to understand them as a process.

Table 4.1: Dynamics of Change

Stage	Description
Denial	Our first reaction to change generally is manifested by feelings such as shock, confusion, and even numbness. It is compounded by disbelief and in some cases may lead to emotional withdrawal.
Resistance	Once reality sets in, we move from feeling numb to being angry and resisting. This is manifested by outbursts, blaming oneself and others, and demonstrating generally uncooperative behaviors. Although the denial phase is more passive, the resistance stage is vocal.
Exploration	This is a turning point at which the shock of change begins to fade away and the mind starts to recognize that the change is here to stay. Behaviors such as asking, learning, and exploring help individuals begin to embrace the change.
Acceptance	Recognizing that the past is gone, and equipped with more information and options, we begin to accept the change. The feelings range from reluctant commitment to utter conviction. With acceptance, individuals begin to formulate a new vision, a clear plan, and compelling goals to move with the change.

Denial is a response to the shock and confusion that hits hard when you don't know what the change will mean for your life and livelihood. During a corporate reorganization, for example, people experience denial as they cope with the sense of powerlessness. Resistance, in contrast, entails anger. It is more vocal than denial and may involve outbursts of blame as emotions are forced to the surface. You feel betrayed. Luckily, you can't fall below the floor, and anger eventually gives way to exploration. You are ready to move on. You activate your support network and begin to feel more positive. You realize that there are opportunities in the new order. Finally, acceptance arises as you learn to accept the new reality. You create goals for yourself and find that you are actually on board.

We go through these stages even when a change is positive. If you've won the lottery, for example, denial is immediate: *I can't believe I've won $10 million.* But anger may also show its face—perhaps when your acquaintances start calling at all hours to ask for money.

Regardless of the situation and our individual response, change takes time. Sometimes we regress, slipping back into denial just when we thought we were enthusiastically exploring the new. Other times we get stuck in a stage and it becomes a stumbling block. Resistance to change is appealing because we think it will allow us to remain in our comfort zone. Regardless of the speed of our progress, recognizing the stages of change helps us go through the emotions. The emotional dynamics of change are illustrated in Figure 4.1.

LEADING PEOPLE THROUGH THE CHANGE CURVE

Even within the change curve shown in Figure 4.1, individual responses to change vary from one person to the next. In fact, we often suggest that leaders categorize how *each* of their team members responds to change. This exercise enables them to prioritize the role that they themselves must play in order to

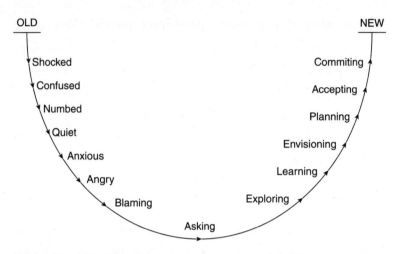

OLD   NEW

Shocked   Commiting
Confused   Accepting
Numbed   Planning
Quiet   Envisioning
Anxious   Learning
Angry   Exploring
Blaming
Asking

Figure 4.1: The Change Curve

help people progress. The categories we use are *Resisters, Late Adapters, Early Adapters,* and *Change Champions.*

Resisters are the skeptical diehards who tend to hold on tight to the status quo. They are trapped in the denial stage; they see absolutely no value in the announced change. In fact, they actively fight the change and may believe that it is designed to benefit only the management ranks.

Early Adapters like to explore change. They ask many questions to examine the nuances of change and test its boundaries. Although they are not always the first to move through the change curve, they are close behind the Change Champions. Early Adapters are adept at kicking the tires of your change plan and offering improvements that save the day. They are good analysts: listen to their ideas and concerns.

The third group, Late Adapters, needs to be encouraged to accept change. They are the fence sitters. This is the camp in which you will see many tentative people hunkering down, waiting to be persuaded one way or the other. Late Adapters need to see that the lines of communication are wide open between management and the wider organization. If you fail to bring them on board, the Resisters will be quick to reel them in.

Finally, Change Champions are known as the innovators and change agents. They are the people on your team who thrive on transformation. They are energized by newness and are on board with the process every step of the way. You should delegate some aspects of the transition to Change Champions, because they need to be constantly engaged and recognized for their efforts and achievements. They tend to be the true catalysts and innovators in the organization. Any attempts to ignore or delay these people can create a rift. In that event, they either will leave the organization or may resist the change because their expectations have been shattered.

The leader has a paramount role in helping people in each of these categories to embrace and commit to change. The following steps provide a roadmap for coaching people in different stages of the curve.

1. *Provide direction:* When someone is stuck in the *denial* stage, leaders need to be more directive. Take the person aside and review in detail what has happened; explain what will happen next. Be specific in terms of what the change means for this individual's role. Begin to urge the person along the path to acceptance.

2. *Be supportive:* Nudging individuals out of the *resistance* stage requires support. They need to know that you understand why they are angry and concerned. Remind them that other people are experiencing these same feelings. Ask questions to find out what is causing the resistance, and help Resisters overcome any logistical barrier they are encountering.

3. *Become a coach:* Assist people who are in the *exploration* stage by coaching them along. Listen to their ideas and tell them what you think. Encourage them to consider how this change might present a new opportunity for them and help them to remain positive. Cheer them on as they become more daring and start to make progress.

4. *Turn Change Champions loose:* Identify the people who have *accepted* the change and assign them challenging projects. Delegate tasks to them, demonstrate your confidence in their abilities, enlist their help to enact the change, increase their responsibilities, and celebrate their successes.

THE CHALLENGE OF CHANGING MANY MINDS

As difficult as it is for each of us to lead with conviction during times of personal change, the complexity is multiplied when we need to transform an entire organization with all of its moving parts. Whether the change entails a small update or a large-scale merger of two public companies, it is always a challenge. After all, companies are made up of people, with varied needs, expectations, and tolerance for risk.

Organizational change is tricky because it alters the balance of power. After all, change frequently ushers in new senior leaders. New faces upset the status quo and leave people at all levels unsure where they stand. When a trusted leader is suddenly gone, people wonder whether they could be next. Likewise, organizational change taps into our career insecurities. It signals a need for new behaviors and skills, which can lower our confidence and self-esteem. People wonder whether they will be able to master the new demands. In addition, senior employees may feel threatened by younger recruits, who can carry out their responsibilities at a much lower pay scale.

The challenges of change become magnified when senior managers leave people in the dark. When an organization fails to communicate the rationale for the change and the desired behaviors for the future, the result is concern and uncertainty. This sows discontent and creates mistrust of the entire change agenda. People perceive the new regime as focusing entirely on creative destruction, with no interest in acknowledging the past. As a result, talented employees begin to explore other options and often exit for better opportunities. This, in many ways, further upsets the delicate balance in the organizational climate.

Another challenge is that change disrupts established systems and norms. People benefit from order and known processes, in general and especially in business. Therefore, when change throws existing systems into question, people tend to block it—and in some cases to sabotage it. Furthermore, if *process* change is difficult, changing an entire *culture* is positively daunting. Cultural change is tricky to achieve, and it seldom sticks. For instance, if an organization has traditionally based promotions on seniority, whereas the new order emphasizes a meritocracy, it will be hard for people to adjust their perceived norm from their years of service to familiar standards of performance. This is especially challenging in large organizations that have relied on tradition to anchor their values, such as state-owned enterprises in China as well as traditional organizations in Japan.

With these challenges to conquer, changing the minds and hearts of many people at once requires a steady hand and a good plan.

One American company that has made a major impact in the Chinese market, as a result of their deft handling of change, is Mary Kay, Inc. To drive their success, the president of Mary Kay China, Paul Mak, launched a large-scale change initiative aimed at transforming how employees perceived themselves and the company. The campaign, geared to engage the female workforce in China, was launched shortly after the company was forced to suspend operations in the country for a time in 1989 because of a government ban on direct selling.

Following the five-month shutdown, Mak launched the initiative to turn Mary Kay employees in China into true believers—in themselves, in the brand, and in balancing their work and personal life. Their stated mission—"reaching out to the heart and spirit of women and enabling personal growth"—engaged thousands of women in China to carry out the mission and values of founder Mary Kay Ash.[2]

Recognized by *Fortune China* as one of the best employers to work for, Mary Kay has been relentless in terms of driving change through ongoing communication, leadership training, talent development, celebrating success, and sharing experiences. The company has established monthly recognition rewards for demonstrating the desired values and behaviors. Making change stick also requires leaders to align employee needs with organizational values. For its part, Mary Kay rewards behaviors that demonstrate integrity, giving, creativity, initiative, and social responsibility.

Thanks to ongoing efforts, the change at Mary Kay China took root. Revenue in China for Mary Kay doubled to $600 million in the three years from 2006 to 2009, and the company said it expects the growth to continue.[3]

Self-Assessment: Mastering the Change Process

Reflect on the changes you are managing, or those you have managed in the past, and circle the frequency with which you engage in the following behaviors. When finished, total your score.

	1	2	3	4	5					
	Hardly ever	Occasionally	Sometimes	Often	Almost always					
1	The rationale for the change is clear to me.					1	2	3	4	5
2	I am personally committed to the change.					1	2	3	4	5
3	I formulate a clear vision for the change.					1	2	3	4	5
4	I communicate the vision constantly and consistently.					1	2	3	4	5
5	I use a mechanism to solicit feedback.					1	2	3	4	5
6	I identify clear milestones and metrics to assess progress.					1	2	3	4	5
7	I identify my Change Champions.					1	2	3	4	5
8	I establish teams working on issues related to the change.					1	2	3	4	5
9	I have identified senior mentors.					1	2	3	4	5
10	I provide ongoing progress reports to my team.					1	2	3	4	5
11	I keep my leader informed.					1	2	3	4	5
12	I earn my leader's support in the change progress.					1	2	3	4	5
13	I recognize the desired behaviors for change.					1	2	3	4	5
14	I celebrate small victories and progress.					1	2	3	4	5
15	I take the time to reflect and manage my stress.					1	2	3	4	5

Add the points to calculate your score.
Total Score: _____
65 or higher = Very Changeable
45–64 = Changeable
44 or lower = Less Chance of Change

SUCCESS MAXIMS FOR ORGANIZATIONAL CHANGE

As the Mary Kay and DFS stories illustrate, leading organizational change successfully entails four fundamental rules of engagement:

1. *Capture the Communication Process.* In the heat of a major change rollout, it is easy to think that everyone knows as much about the change as you do. But that's never the case. The worst mistake you can make is to remain silent. In fact, we tell leaders to remember to *over*communicate. If the wider organization is not kept in the loop, naysayers cluster and subcultures start to proliferate. These subcultures strengthen the resistance to change and create resentment; often their narrative of reality becomes stronger than your own, and you find yourself competing for airtime.

This is what happened to the auto industry in Detroit in 2008 and 2009, when it was teetering on the brink of bankruptcy amidst the government bailouts of General Motors and Chrysler. Industry leaders recognized the need for change. They even knew what they needed to do—create smaller, greener cars to combat rising gasoline prices. In short, they needed to completely separate themselves from the past. Where they failed was in maintaining an elitist attitude and a blind distrust of unions. Unlike Mary Kay China, they were unable to communicate a persuasive vision for change. In the end, the unions became a greater enemy of the car companies than the competition. In the absence of an interactive voice from leadership, the unions overpowered management and forced through their agenda. The unions won and the auto industry nearly collapsed.

2. *Disrupt Systems.* Change can't stick unless the leader disrupts existing systems. Tampering with conventional ways of operating is a high-risk proposition when a company has been successful, but any change requires a reexamination of process.

At DFS, as part of their transformation from discount retailer to luxury boutique, they reworked the structure in order to create greater consistency from store to store. Because DFS was a product of a completely decentralized structure, with decision making and development happening locally until the late '90s, every outlet was a bit different from the rest. Given this opportunity to start from scratch once he became president of worldwide operations, Michael Schriver decided to create a whole new formula that catered to pleasing the upscale clientele in the LVMH family of businesses. They inverted the pyramid by pushing management closer to the sales floor. They adjusted their jobs so that the role was no longer administrative but rather in service of customers. They also moved the voice of the customer closer to buyers for the first time by encouraging floor managers to interact directly with buyers.

As they redesigned systems and recast roles to have greater customer focus, they always asked the question: does this fit with our strategy or does it not? They put a relentless focus on catering to the luxury equation.

3. *Invest in Training.* Great leaders invest in people. Radical changes in focus, such as the one DFS planned, require a significant investment in training the workforce. Because in the past change efforts had withered and died at DFS, there was a certain amount of initial skepticism throughout the organization. Diehard resisters to the change thought they could wait it out, just as they had before. But the previous training efforts had been minimal, whereas Schriver went whole hog. He designed a series of shared learning experiences in which hundreds of people were gathered in multiple locations to learn what it meant to be in the luxury business and deliver a great customer experience. They reinforced the message with repeated workshops and hands-on training sessions.

Change also requires a coaching mentality. At DFS they completely redesigned their training program for sales associates. They launched an "apprentice to master" career path that emphasized mentorship and a staged advancement process that was fully transparent.

4. *Know Where Your People Are.* It is important to understand where people stand with the change. Are they on board? If not, why not? And what can be done? Schriver led the change effort with his own personal behavior. He implemented 360° feedback for all managers, starting with himself. The company engaged in an ongoing, honest dialogue. They expected people to push back and problem solve. Management listened to concerns and fielded the tough questions. The only thing that was less welcome than naysayers at DFS was passive

acceptance. The idea was to allow individuals to pressure test the new ways of working in order to make them better and stronger. As a result, instead of being change victims, the DFS workforce became actively engaged.

Best Practices for Change

Our work with DFS and numerous other organizations has resulted in a set of best practices aimed at helping leaders expedite an effective and fruitful change process.

Lead change by example: Recognize where we are on the change curve and determine what steps you need to take in order to lead the change with conviction. You need to be fully committed to the change, because people will take cues from your actions and demeanor.

Solicit feedback: Find out how people are feeling about the change and get their ideas for improvements. For example, launch a climate survey in order to assess people's attitudes, opinions, and feelings toward the change. Include all levels of the organization. As you gauge reactions to the change, try to speak less and listen more. This feedback will help you crystallize your vision for change and plan the appropriate course of action.

Formulate a clear and compelling vision for the future: This vision should include the rationale for change and provide the inspiration needed to rally the troops. Utilize clear goals that appeal to the mind and capture the heart.

Overcommunicate: Conduct intensive sessions (with people at all levels) to communicate the change, report on progress, solicit feedback, and enable people to express themselves by sharing their own narratives.

Include Change Champions: Establish teams from across departments and charge them with managing the change initiative in areas ranging from operations improvement to organizational restructuring. Have these teams report back to senior leadership periodically. Assign a senior leader for each team to act as a sponsor.

Engage stakeholders: Set up meetings with key stakeholders (that is, board, customers, regulatory agencies) to update them on progress and solicit feedback and suggestions.

Recognize achievements: Reward role models and celebrate victories. This will help ensure that the desired behaviors and values are demonstrated throughout the organization. Recognizing achievements will institutionalize the change, instill a sense of excitement about it, and demonstrate the sincerity of senior leadership.

To make change stick, leaders must have an unwavering conviction and a strong sense of determination. Every great transformation, without exception, has its highs and lows, its peak performers and disappointments. Regardless of the challenges, leaders can't lose faith or retreat to their old place of comfort. Short-term failures are a requisite part of every change effort; keeping an eye on the prize and celebrating small wins are the markers of resilience. Change, after all, is the ongoing job of every leader. It is how organizations keep pace with the needs of customers and remain ahead of competitors. As the saying goes, failure is not falling down, but refusing to get back up.

Five Guiding Principles for Leading Change:

1. Accept change as constant.
2. Look at change as an opportunity to explore and learn.
3. Before you act, examine your reaction to change and assess your readiness.
4. Help others to go through the change by involving, teaching, probing, and inspiring them.
5. Encourage ideas and enable people to express themselves.

5

The Pillar of Conflict

The most intense conflicts, if overcome, leave behind a sense of security and calm that is not easily disturbed. It is just these intense conflicts which are needed to produce valuable and lasting results.

—Carl Jung

Conflict can be a useful tool for creating dynamic tension. However, if that tension is not effectively managed it can yield disastrous results. Such was the case in a service-based company in the Mid-Atlantic region. The CEO, who we will call Joseph, had been an administrator in higher education after graduating from college. It was in that environment that he learned the benefits of generating creative tension through conflict. His experience at the university carried over into the business world, and he used these techniques to manage departments as he progressed up the corporate ladder. In time, he was offered the opportunity to lead a business that was being spun off from the corporate parent he worked for. The business, though fundamentally solid, took on considerable debt in the spin-off.[1]

The new executive team was a diverse group. Some had worked at the parent company for a long time prior to the spin-off. Others were industry experts who were hired from other companies to help grow the business. Still other hires were functional specialists who had no experience at all in the industry. As for Joseph, he used what had worked for him in the past. He cultivated differing opinions in the executive suite and encouraged arguments that occasionally escalated into shouting matches. This approach seemed to work for Joseph, at least for a while, until rapid consolidation and global competition brought massive change to the industry. In the wake of such turbulence, the company needed a unified approach. That's when the business ran into trouble.

Unfortunately, Joseph's leadership style proved to be problematic at this critical juncture. Encouraging conflicts and allowing them to develop into sharp public discord backfired, and his team lost confidence in his authority. In this challenging new business environment, the executives found a lot to fight about, and decisions were made haphazardly. Conflicts remained unresolved, and tensions spilled over and distracted the entire organization. Infighting ensued, and the business collapsed within five years.

An organization's success or failure can depend on management's ability to handle differences constructively. The pressure to achieve objectives, and the inevitable challenges of team dynamics, make escalating tensions an inescapable part of the mix. But, as the case of Food Flight shows, conflict requires deliberate management. Leaders must be in a position to address discord before it destroys trust, damages relationships, and negatively affects business. As we will see, dealing with conflict constructively is a trade-off: short-term pain for a long-term gain.

Leading with conviction requires a mind-set that allows one to actively manage conflict. Great leaders can't and don't shy away from the challenge.

CONFLICT IS A GROWTH INDUSTRY

Conflict is inevitable. In fact, the prevailing winds of change have turned conflict into a growth industry. Where is this ubiquitous conflict coming from? Technological change, just one source, has given rise to disruptive business models. New ways of working have challenged the status quo in dozens of industries, from consumer retail to media. As a result, new competitors emerge from out of nowhere. This requires a fast response from teams that are nimble, diverse, and willing to experiment. In addition, the rise of China and the other populous economic superpowers in Asia and elsewhere have fixed the world's attention on markets that are entirely different from their own. Opening offices in opposing time zones, with employees spread across the globe and speaking several different languages, requires an entirely new mind-set with regard to resources, priorities, and profit. We are working in multigenerational teams, in entirely new ways, and in places that are unlike any we are accustomed to. Navigating global differences and cultural norms can be a full-time job. Finally, technology has brought customers much closer to the business, with social media options such as Twitter making shareholder activism more prevalent and customer feedback instantaneous. The upshot is that we are being forced to abandon our comfort zones.

On the one hand, as we saw with Food Flight International, when conflict is left unchecked the lack of understanding can result in second-guessing and mistrust. An inability to address conflict is costly in terms of focus and effectiveness. On the other hand, skillfully addressing conflict without attacking anyone's self-esteem transforms thorny situations into learning experiences. As Jeff Weiss and Jonathan Hughes of Vantage Partners point out in the *Harvard Business Review*, "Clashes between parties are the crucibles in which creative solutions are developed and wise trade-offs among competing objectives are made. So instead of simply trying to reduce disagreements, senior executives need to embrace conflict and, just as important, institutionalize mechanisms for managing it."[2]

Leading with conviction requires that you act from a place of empathy and good intentions. On that basis, resolving conflicts can take an organization to the next level. An executive we worked with at Aetna, Roy Vander Putten, illustrated this point perfectly.

An officer and employee of Aetna Life and Casualty Company for twenty-six years, Vander Putten was appointed CEO of an organization called Executive Risk, Inc. (ERI) in 1988. Officially launched in 1987, ERI was a joint venture formed by Aetna to underwrite executive board liability. When Vander Putten became CEO, the company had fourteen employees and $38 million in gross premiums. In less than ten years, they built the business to 309 employees and $292 million in gross premiums written. ERI went public in 1994, and its stock price soared from $12 to a high of $75 per share.[3] Vander Putten, along with the company's president, Stephen Sills, was the force who propelled ERI's growth. The company's success was due, in part, to exceptional leadership and an expert handling of the conflicts that arose as the business rapidly expanded.

Achieving success at a fast and furious pace, as ERI did, is seldom a neat and tidy process. In fact, discord arose in the executive suite just as the IPO was starting to heat up. The senior team was small, and egos clashed under the mounting pressure. Two of Vander Putten's key executives became particularly antagonistic toward each other. The finance lead was very focused on numbers and analytics, whereas a human resources VP was preoccupied with talent management and recruiting. Their worldviews were in stark opposition, as were their interests.

As tension mounted between the two, Vander Putten became aware of the potentially explosive situation and took the entire management team away on a weekend corporate retreat. At the beginning of the event, the two were publicly caustic, and each seemed ready to walk out. A verbal altercation between the executives created a scene during one of the dinners, and Vander Putten interceded to defuse the situation.

The next day, during the weekend's team-building exercises, he paired the two up together. They were red-faced at having to interact, and things seemed destined to end badly. But then something clicked. Forced to collaborate in an environment where the stakes were low, they were able to see that their opposing styles were actually complementary. Working together, with Vander Putten as an active mediator, they became a solid team. After that day, the two built a rapport and were able to use their differences in a productive way.

Conflict is normal and necessary. In fact, Carl Jung believed that conflict, if addressed successfully, could deepen the quality of a relationship. Vander Putten stepped into the mediator's role and transformed the situation at a critical moment in ERI's history. Yet because many of us have been taught to remain passive or neutral in the face of conflict, this leadership pillar is difficult to cultivate.

SOURCES OF CONFLICT

The two leading sources of conflict in a marriage are reported to be finances and parenting styles. Couples argue over mounting debts and spending habits, just as they do about important family decisions. Organizations have their own common triggers that cause conflict. The sources of tension within organizations are varied, but the majority of conflicts spring from unfulfilled or differing expectations.

Although differences between employees and teams are not a bad thing, they need to be actively managed. One of the roles of the leader is to anticipate substantive conflicts and determine how to intercede before they turn into crises that distract people and disrupt business. The following are the sources of friction we see most often within groups.

Misalignment of Priorities and Values

The failure to agree on goals and priorities is a primary conflict trigger. Sometimes a misalignment of expectations is created when companies hand down goals without clarifying the rationale behind them—leading individuals to draw their own conclusions. Other times misalignment occurs as geographic and cultural boundaries melt down and differing worldviews are exposed. In this case, tension is the result of conflicting norms and values. In nations such as China, for example, contracts are not treated with the same deference or legal adherence that they receive in many other countries, whereas formality in other areas, such as showing deep respect for elders, is expected in nations such as China and Japan, much more so than elsewhere. Within organizations, these types of inconsistencies in terms of norms and values can lead to frustration and conflict.

Constraints and High Stakes

Constraints such as time pressure create stress that can escalate into conflict. We see this most frequently during the seasonal or annual peaks in organizational workflow that are associated with deadlines, such as quarter-end and the closing of a tax or fiscal year. In the case of ERI, mentioned earlier, the conflict between executives was intensified as the company's initial public offering approached. Interdependence multiplies the potential for conflict; for example, when one individual's failure to meet goals or deadlines puts another person's success in jeopardy. As stakes and stress increase, so does the potential for conflict.

Similarly, failing to meet goals altogether sparks conflict that takes the shape of blame shifting. Unfulfilled expectations often have associated consequences that people scramble to avoid. Blame and the avoidance of blame both generate conflict.

Conflicting Interests

Similar to misalignment, conflicting interests arise when resources or other material interests are in dispute. Following a car accident, for example, an insurance company may need to investigate—eventually denying payment on certain claims. It is in the financial interest of the insurance company to pay fewer claims, but a customer's interest is served when his claim is fulfilled. In this case, denying compensation improves profit for the insurer but decreases customer satisfaction, loyalty, and trust.

Conflicting interests are also evident when municipalities or nations compete for power, economic advantage, and natural resources. For example, China's environmental record in some categories has created tension with neighboring countries and with much of the rest of the world. China has responded with increasing environmental regulations, which have led to some improvements. No country in history has emerged as a major industrial power without creating a legacy of environmental damage, and China is no exception.

Clearly, conflicting interests will always be a source of friction between nations. These conflicts are particularly thorny because both parties can make the case that their actions and perspectives are appropriate for their citizens. And refusal to approach conflicts as an opportunity to explore win-win solutions can only prolong the conflict and its resulting damage.

Change and Disruption

Change creates conflict for several reasons. First, it awakens our natural fear of the unknown and forces us out of our comfort zone, thereby causing stress and elevating tension. Next, change within organizations often signals a power shift. Regime changes create conflict when power struggles occur and loyalties are tested. Finally, change creates conflict because people are unclear about expectations, which often shift when things are in flux. Think about the times when you have felt the most conflicted. Chances are they occurred during the times in your life when you were experiencing personal or professional change.

Personality Differences

Conflicts also occur when miscommunication and misunderstanding create a lack of trust between individuals. Managers and subordinates may not see eye to eye, for example, leaving both parties feeling wary, uncertain and even threatened. A one-size-fits-all leadership approach is another culprit. For example, an engaged, hands-on leadership style may appeal to less-experienced colleagues who require specific direction, but that same approach may feel like micromanagement to a more experienced and independent colleague.

Personal Crisis

Conflicts arise as the result of personal problems that can adversely affect an individual's work performance and office relationships. Because we are accustomed to keeping personal issues to ourselves, changes in behavior may be misinterpreted by colleagues, who jump to the wrong conclusion and take it personally.

Leadership Failure

Sometimes the source of conflict is none other than the leaders themselves. Ivan Graham, a London-based marketing executive, was a driven individual in search of new challenges. When a well-known Chinese company offered him a job in Shanghai, he jumped at the opportunity—in part because Graham would have a larger role, in which he would manage a multi-million-dollar RMB ad campaign and launch the company's digital marketing initiatives. When he finally arrived in Shanghai, Graham discovered, much to his surprise, that the company had already soft-launched a digital marketing initiative, something his boss had never told him about in their negotiations. This created tension: Graham believed that it was his job to spearhead the initiative, whereas Xinghan Jing, the Chinese executive who had begun the rollout (and hadn't been briefed about Graham's role), tried to cut Graham out. Neither one of the two was to blame here—the fault lay squarely with David's boss, who hadn't bothered to tie up loose ends and didn't step in to resolve the situation when it started to escalate. The conflict was further exacerbated when the boss started to publicly berate the Chinese employees in team meetings, saying that the four or five expatriate workers they had were miles ahead of the locals. This unnecessarily widened not only the chasm between Graham and Mr. Xinghan, but also the one between expatriate and Chinese employees, leading to further conflicts in the organization.

Another leadership faux pas is sweeping conflict under the carpet. Most leaders don't want to embarrass anyone, especially themselves, so they pretend the conflict doesn't exist. This is what happened at a start-up we've worked with, after a junior manager complained that he was being bullied by a senior executive. Both were considered to be star employees, and the organization couldn't afford to lose either. The manager brought this to the attention of the bosses several times, but they did not want to rock the boat. The situation continued to simmer for a long time and eventually blew up when security cameras caught the executive snooping through important documents on the manager's desk. The resulting showdown was unpleasant, to say the least.

When there is a conflict, the tendency is for people to avoid engaging in dialogue. We are simply not trained or emotionally equipped to engage in difficult conversations, and so we resort to avoidance. In some cases, people will even resort to complete silence to avoid being part of the conflict and to bypass the storm of emotion that may arise from any conflict.

When leaders fail to intercede, however, tensions escalate and one of the parties eventually explodes "out of the blue." To avoid this type of disruption, leaders need to be prepared with a plan to manage and resolve conflict.

APPROACHES TO CONFLICT

Conflict in and of itself is neither good nor bad; it is how we deal with the situation that determines whether it is disruptive or constructive.[4]

In the 1970s, Kenneth Thomas and Ralph Kilmann developed the Thomas-Kilmann Conflict Mode Instrument (TKI), a tool designed to measure an individual's response to conflict situations. As part of that work, they identified five main styles for dealing with conflict that vary in their degree of cooperativeness and assertiveness. Their premise is that people typically have a preferred conflict resolution style. However, they also note that different styles are most useful in different situations. Figure 5.1 illustrates Thomas and Kilmann's styles.

When people *compete* in order to resolve a conflict, it transforms the situation into a zero-sum game: I win, you lose—or vice versa. This mind-set implies that you are seeking to maintain your position at the expense of the other party. Competition as an approach to conflict is best suited to situations where the outcome of the conflict is more important to you than the relationship with your opponent. If the conflict

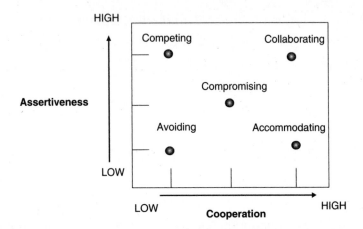

Figure 5.1: Thomas-Kilmann Conflict-Handling Modes

Source: From "Conflict and Negotiation Process in Organizations" by K. Thomas. Copyright 1992 by L. M. Hough. Adapted by permission.[5]

is with an industry rival, for example, with each side competing for the same business, then this approach suits the situation. However, if the conflict is with a close colleague or customer, a competitive stance won't lead to an appropriate resolution in most cases.

Accommodation, another approach to conflict, requires setting aside your own needs in order to acquiesce to the other person's requests or demands. This is another zero-sum tactic— I lose, you win. Accommodation is appropriate when you place a high value on the relationship, and if the outcome of the conflict is of little importance to you but is highly important to the other party. Most of us will choose to acquiesce to the wishes of our boss, or perhaps to our spouse, but are less willing to accommodate a colleague, particularly when the stakes of the conflict are high for us.

When you sidestep or withdraw altogether from a conflict, you are choosing *avoidance*. Although this is a very common response to disagreements, when you ignore or postpone conflict it remains unresolved and neither party walks away feeling fully satisfied. However, avoidance is a suitable alternative in situations in which all other options are unsatisfactory. For example, if the relationship *and* winning are equally important to you, you may need to avoid the conflict until a suitable resolution presents itself.

One of the most common approaches to conflict is *compromise*. It is a relatively low-risk approach in terms of a possible escalation of tensions, but it also does not fully put a stake in the ground or get to the root of the issue. Compromise de-escalates the conflict quickly and efficiently by seeking a fair and equitable split between the two positions. It allows you to preserve the relationship by demonstrating goodwill and also lets you claim something of a win. For this resolution to stick, both parties must be flexible and willing to settle on the major issues. Compromise is a good option when, as is often the case in the political arena, the stakes are very high for both parties.

Finally, *collaboration* is the I-win-and-you-win approach. It involves cooperating with the other party to try to resolve a common issue to a mutually satisfying outcome. Each side must feel that the outcomes gained through collaboration are better than what they could achieve on their own.

Collaboration often requires mediation as well as preexisting goodwill between the parties. Collaboration can work in resolving conflicts with colleagues, partners, customers, and even competitors. In the best of cases, collaboration leads to an improved relationship as well as a positive outcome for both parties. It does require mutual respect and trust. In their absence, collaboration rarely works.

A Way to Collaborate

Collaboration, the win-win approach to conflict, is often difficult to do because it requires patience, emotional intelligence, creative thinking, and time. Should you choose to collaborate to resolve a conflict, the following framework will assist you:

1. Avoid your tendency to react and rush to judgment.
2. Know what you want and be clear on the outcome.
3. Put yourself in the other person's shoes and empathize with that person's needs.
4. Explore options and develop creative solutions.
5. Select the right solution and develop a mutual agreement.
6. Follow through on your commitment.
7. Continue to build and sustain the relationship.

Table 5.1: Comparison Analysis of Thomas-Kilmann Conflict-Handling Modes

Your Approach	Your Position	Supporting Rationale	Potential Issues
Competing	I must get my way.	I am committed to it.	The other party might feel defeated or humiliated.
Accommodating	My position is not as important.	Harmony is top priority.	You might be taken advantage of.
Avoiding	I don't want to get involved.	Too much pain.	The problem does not get addressed.
Compromising	Let's come up with something workable.	Prolonged conflicts must be avoided.	Expediency in exchange for effectiveness.
Collaborating	Expanding the possibility.	Quality outcome and ongoing relationship are possible.	Time, maturity, and trust.

Source: Adapted by permission. Copyright 1992 by L. M. Hough.[6]

Each of the Thomas-Kilmann Conflict-Handling Modes has its own tradeoffs, as presented in Table 5.1.

BETWEEN ISLANDS, BUILD BRIDGES: A FRAMEWORK FOR EFFECTIVE CONFLICT RESOLUTION

Regardless of precisely how you approach conflict, leading with conviction requires that you step into the role of mediator.

Meeting conflict head-on, with a plan, can foster goodwill and turn difficult situations into opportunities to forge stronger relationships.

For example, consider the case of Bingxin Zhang, the thirty-three-year-old CEO of Kubao Information Technology Co. Ltd., a large mobile game developer in China. With hundreds of young employees all competing fiercely in this fast-paced industry, opportunities for conflicts abound at Kubao. In addition, because game design is such a collaborative field, conflicts can have a profoundly negative effect on productivity. With this in mind, Zhang and his team have devised an innovative approach to maintaining harmony. Their process is as novel as it is effective.

Using gaming elements as the basis of their philosophy, the employees are invited to log on to a website every day after work and rate their happiness on a scale of 1–100. If an employee reports a low rating, their HR representative steps in to help. In fact, someone meets with the employee the very next day to determine how to resolve the issues. Whether the problem is workload, interpersonal discord, or a creative disagreement, the company intercedes in order to maintain a high level of morale. According to Zhang, employees are happier just knowing the company is engaged and interested in their satisfaction. On most days, the majority of workers report a high rating. Zhang says that they save their distress calls for times when they need company intervention. Above all, the system provides a fast and effective way to manage conflicts before they escalate.

Regardless of whether your plan is as proactive and innovative as what Zhang put together, there are certain guidelines that should be built into your approach for leading through conflict. These steps, which we use in our coaching sessions, can be adapted and used as a roadmap for conflict resolution. This method presumes that you, as the leader, can remain objective, and that your goal is to defuse a difficult situation between employees.

1. Root Out the Source of Conflict

The cause of conflict between two or more people is often hidden below the surface. The parties may tell you that the issue is about a budgeting shortfall, for example, when in reality it goes deeper. Conflict, in many cases, is a symptom rather than the initial trigger. In fact, there are often weeks or months of simmering resentment before a conflict actually erupts. Even if the parties don't readily admit or understand the true source of their conflict, do your best to help them uncover the truth.

In the case of Roy Vander Putten's ERI, the loss of trust between the two executives went back a long time. Many months prior to the IPO, one of the two had "called the other out" publicly in a way that was embarrassing. After that, the conflict escalated, slowly but surely, reaching a fever pitch when the stress of the IPO started to make matters worse. When the two managed to discuss the problem off-site, the misunderstanding was resolved. To get individuals to open up, you need to probe carefully. Ask neutral questions without resorting to interrogation.

2. Be Committed to Resolution

Conflicts can sometimes seem intractable, but you must remain focused on a solution even if others believe that all is lost. In Vander Putten's case, both individuals were threatening to walk out, believing that they were at an impasse. The surprise solution presented itself because of Vander Putten's resolve. He was able to bring the parties together and refocus their efforts on one thing—making the organization successful. The key is to see both sides of the issue. In his book *Leading Through Conflict*, Mark Gerzon talks about the idea of "Integral Vision." Gerzon says that the mediator must "be a witness who sees the total picture" and "hold a vision of the entire conflict, with all of its divisions and consequences."[7]

3. Enable People to Express Themselves

Allowing people to interact with each other, openly and honestly, helps them to feel heard and see the common ground that exists between them. More than that, expressing feelings and concerns is empowering and in many ways healing. Psychologists, after all, are well paid to enable people to express themselves.

With that in mind, it is important to encourage active listening and respect. If one party is waiting for a turn to speak instead of listening, then your job is to get the parties to engage in a dialogue and empathize with each other. Sometimes the simple act of talking through the problem can provide a certain closure. This brings to mind the story of a woman who came before a traffic judge in London. She had been on her way to an appointment when she made a right turn at an intersection. There was a "No Right Turn" sign, but it was covered in graffiti, rendering it illegible. A police officer pulled her over and gave her a ticket without allowing her to explain the situation. When she arrived in court the judge read the report and dismissed the ticket immediately. He had seen this sign before. Yet the woman refused to leave. She insisted on having a full hearing. "I didn't come here to have the ticket dismissed," she said. She had come to talk, and she was not about to leave without being heard.

Establishing a dialogue in which both parties listen and feel heard can go a long way toward solving the conflict.

4. Facilitate the Process

Your responsibility as leader is to help resolve the conflict so that everyone can go back to focusing on his or her primary job. That means managing your own emotions and being objective and authoritative. You should be firm and assertive while also remembering that there are egos at the center of the conflict. Listen closely to what each person is saying and observe body language. What you say and how you say it can turn the tide of the conversation. For example:

- Safeguard information—keep the details of the interaction confidential.
- Accentuate the positive behaviors expressed by all parties.
- Demonstrate superb listening skills.
- Demonstrate compassion, mutual respect, and flexibility.
- Explore options and agree on outcomes.
- Bring people together to discuss conflicts before they fester.
- Instill a culture of openness in which people challenge each other.
- When conflicts are resolved, celebrate occasionally.

5. Follow Up to Ensure a Lasting Resolution

The objective of follow-up is to make sure the resolution is effective and lasting. Your involvement, even after the conflict is settled, sends a signal to both parties that you expect them to abide by the agreement and work together in a constructive way. Because the conflict is likely to have subsided by this point, this step is easy to shrug off. Don't do that; skipping the follow-up may lead to another escalation of tensions.

THE UPSIDE OF CONFLICT

We've spent the chapter describing the role of the leader in conflict resolution. In closing, we'll note that the least-explored role of the leader in managing conflict is to knowing how and when to allow conflict to flourish. From our perspective, conflict can act as a positive force in an organization under three conditions.

First, conflict is a tool for leading change. Conflict forces people out of their safety zones and can be a catalyst for finding novel and creative solutions. Innovation, after all, very often springs from adversity.

Second, conflicts can force us to examine all sides of an issue. If managed properly, conflict can open one's eyes to how other people perceive complex issues. In this way, conflict has the potential to turn adversaries into allies.

Finally, conflict can lead to honest communication. In an age when most of us spend our days sitting before a computer screen and communicating by email and instant message, conflict can cause individuals to face each other and truly interact.

Five Guiding Principles for Conflict Resolution:

1. Perceive conflict as an opportunity to air issues and deepen the quality of relationships.

2. Facilitate a discussion in which the focus is on both the logical and the emotional side of the conflict.
3. Address conflict immediately; don't let it fester.
4. Establish conflict resolution as an integral part of your value system.
5. Remain composed and positive as the storms of emotions and accusations run their course.

6

The Pillar of Creativity

Creativity is a skill that never goes out of style.

—Larry Rosenstoek

We all read articles about creative organizations—such as Google, Apple, Procter & Gamble, and 3M—that make headlines with their innovative products and services. However, one of the cases we use in training classes, to start conversation about creativity, is not a traditional business at all but a restaurant that was based in Spain for its twenty-five-plus-year history.

Roses is a nondescript town overlooking the azure waters of the Mediterranean at Cata Montjoi in Catalonia, Spain. Connoisseurs of fine food descended on this little town from all over the world—landing in Barcelona and then undertaking a two-hour road journey to Roses. Thanks to celebrity chef Ferran Adrià, the driving force behind the iconic Michelin three-star restaurant El Bulli, Roses was on the map of the world's top gourmet destinations.

It was not easy to get a table at El Bulli—you might have had to wait for as long as seven years to get a dinner reservation. Some desperate diners had been known to make all kinds of excuses—"This will be my final birthday"—to get a reservation.[1] And the meal, when you finally got a chance to savor it, did not disappoint. It was a five-hour-long gastronomical journey that no diner could ever forget. Adrià tantalized your taste buds with as many as forty-three courses, each one painstakingly put together in such a way that it preserved the purity of the original flavors. Adrià's goal was to turn the meal into an experience that engaged all five senses. Just as an artist experiments with hues, brushstrokes, and media, Adrià experimented with flavors, textures, and combinations. It was not for nothing that *Gourmet* magazine called Adrià "the Salvador Dali of the kitchen."

Cooking, to Adrià, was not just about food or the simple act of eating—it was the blending of inspiration, imagination, and invention. Adrià and his team seemed to have hit on a winning formula to unlock creativity, which explains El Bulli's astounding success. From 1987—three years after Adrià took over El Bulli—the restaurant stayed open for only six months out of the year; the other six were spent immersed in creativity, concocting imaginative new dishes. According to a government brochure, "Ferran and his team deconstructed and recon-figured culinary and gastronomic conventions by observing the constituent parts of cooking in a critical and analytical way in order to establish new relationships between previously uncon-nected components."[2] Over the years, Adrià experimented with influences such as Mediterranean-inspired haute cuisine principles,[3] deconstruction, minimalism, avant-garde cooking, "sixth-sense dishes,"[4] dishes with influences from Japan, and science (through the use of liquid nitrogen and calcium chlo-ride).[5] The experimentation paid off—El Bulli was a runaway success featured on most lists of the best restaurants in the world.

El Bulli could have been just another small-town fine dining restaurant. A near-fanatic emphasis on creativity is what accounts for El Bulli's meteoric rise. Adrià saw himself not as a chef, but as the creative director. During the six months when the restaurant was closed, his core team scoured the globe for new ideas. "[Adrià's team of chefs] work almost telepathically, travelling together all over the world during the six months of frenetic creativity when El Bulli shuts, sitting down at restau-rants in San Francisco, Bangkok, Tokyo, Shanghai—some-times a dozen different sittings a day—gathering ideas, coming up with new ones and, as Adrià said, 'working, working all the time, drinking nothing but water.'"[6] The team experimented with new techniques, concepts, and products, and every exper-iment was painstakingly documented at the El Bulli workshop in Barcelona, the restaurant's version of a corporate R&D center. The creations from this workshop were further refined in El Bulli's kitchen. And Adrià believed in measuring creativity—something he did by cataloguing the inventions. "At El Bulli we created a concept—creative audit. We are able to analyze what has been created in the off season," Adrià said during a talk at Google.[7]

Dubbed by *Time* magazine "the most influential restaurant in the world," El Bulli's grand next act is planned for 2014, when it will reopen as a foundation dedicated to culinary creativity.

As Ferran Adrià illustrates, building a pillar of creativity is one way that outstanding leaders differentiate themselves from the rest. Within an organization, it's the difference between Apple Inc. and the much less successful Motorola, which struggled mightily leading up to its 2011 sale to Google. According to a 2010 study from Ernst & Young, the ability to manage, organize, cultivate, and nurture creative thinking and innovation is directly linked to growth and achievement.[8]

If we define innovation as a leader's capacity to harness and commercialize new ideas, one fundamental element of that capability is creative thinking. Despite the urgent need in our world for creative solutions to complex problems, it is only in the last decade or so that the creative process has become a popular topic of research. However, Teresa Amabile, a professor at Harvard Business School and author of *The Progress Principle* and other landmark works, has conducted research on creativity for over thirty years and is arguably the preeminent scholar on the topic. According to Amabile, "creativity depends on the right people working in the right environment." She notes that creativity takes a serious hit in times when organizations are lean, "stretching fewer employees to cover ever more work."[9]

Still, research shows that creativity and innovation are on the minds of leaders today. A survey of 1,600 executives by the Boston Consulting Group found that creativity and innovation have been moving up on the strategic agenda of companies in recent years.[10] The study, conducted in 2010, found that after a moderate retrenchment, companies are recommitting to pursuing innovation. "They have pushed it back to the top of their priority lists and plan to boost their innovation spending—despite the [in 2010] stagnant economy."[11] Still, the report suggested that companies in mature economies are comparatively tentative in terms of their investment in innovation. The report warned that "emerging" economies—such as China, India, and Brazil—are placing an even greater emphasis on promoting innovation as a way to grow and compete.

In our work, we have found that the key to forging a pillar of creativity, in any organization, is incorporating it into the mix of a company's key values. The emphasis here is on *mix;* fostering innovation need not be an extreme endeavor that forces out analysis and rigor. However, because most leaders still heavily favor hard skills that can be consistently measured—such as finance and marketing—there is work to be done to authentically bring innovation into the list of priorities. We will look at two broad tactics, *fostering creativity* and *embracing difference*, as two ways to open the doors to innovative thinking by leaders.

FOSTERING CREATIVITY

We know that building a pillar of creativity is essential for leading organizations into the future, yet we also know that the mind, by nature, is more comfortable with routines. Creativity requires change, and change challenges the mind's natural inclination toward stability and predictability. Therefore leaders need to first explore their comfort zone in terms of creativity, then develop the ability to adapt their thinking to meet new and emerging demands, and finally nurture in others that same self-knowledge and openness to change.

The need for leaders to embrace creativity is not an academic challenge, but a reality we must face. The economic storm sweeping across the developed economies and the increasing stress on Chinese companies to become more innovative are further reasons to pay attention to the right side of the brain, which is responsible for insight and creativity. While some leaders are rethinking their processes and their job descriptions with creativity in mind, others still tend to see it as a distraction.

Embracing change through creative thinking can result in both higher productivity and greater job satisfaction. To realize these benefits, leaders from business and the public sector must develop the mental flexibility to shift between reason and discovery, analysis and insight, short-term and long-term perspectives, and strategic and tactical goals, and strike a balance between blue-sky thinking and delivering results.

Recognizing that imagination is the gateway to break-throughs in science and technology, researchers are collecting relevant data on the physiological and psychological factors underlying creativity. Likewise, through brain imaging and careful observation of the interaction of neurons, scientists over the last decade have accumulated an impressive body of work on the brain and the dynamics of breakthrough thinking.

Advances in neuroscience have also fueled popular inter-est in thinking and creativity. For example, the book *Iconoclast: A Neuroscientist Reveals How to Think Differently*—by the dis-tinguished American neuroeconomist Gregory S. Berns, direc-tor of the Center for Neuropolicy at Emory University—is both a fascinating journey into the mind and a revealing look at the challenges facing individuals and organizations in lever-aging insight and creativity. Berns notes that the brain has three natural roadblocks that stand in the way of innovative think-ing: flawed perception, fear of failure, and the inability to persuade others. For most of us, our habits and established patterns of thinking have a way of discouraging creative inquiry, keeping us nestled in our zones of comfort. Berns demonstrates that creativity is not a gift possessed by the lucky few; rather, it's a variety of distinct thought processes that we all can learn to use more effectively.[12]

Psychology researcher and professor Robert Epstein agrees that creativity can be cultivated. In fact, he has conducted research showing that strengthening certain skill sets leads to an increase in novel ideas. His findings indicate that focused effort, such as seeking out new challenges and broadening your

119

knowledge in fields outside of your own, can open the flood-gates for creativity.[13] "As strange as it sounds, creativity can become a habit," agrees researcher Jonathan Plucker, PhD, a psychology professor at Indiana University. "Making it one helps you become more productive."[14]

As the experiences of many creative organizations show us, many of the best ideas today emerge at the intersection of disciplines. "[An] explosion of remarkable ideas is what happened in Florence during the Renaissance, and it suggests something very important. If we can just reach an intersection of disciplines or cultures, we will have a greater chance of innovating, simply because there are so many unusual ideas to go around," wrote Frans Johansson in his book *The Medici Effect.*[15]

Moreover, Johansson notes that creativity needn't always be about complicated ideas and major investments. Sometimes it is about pure ingenuity. Consider the case of a large soap manufacturer in China that was facing a logistical problem at its main plant. As the individual blocks of soap travelled down the conveyor belt, a machine would swoop down and wrap them in paper in one swift move. However, the machine was also sealing some empty wrappers into neat rectangular boxes. This was a problem because those empty boxes would then move ahead on the same conveyor belt and be packed into cartons, ready to be shipped to retailers. Flooded with complaints, senior management was stymied. Try as they might, they couldn't come up with a solution that didn't require a huge investment. Then one of the plant workers came up with the solution: to position a fan close to the conveyor belt just before the soap was to be packed into cartons. The fan would blow away the empty wrappers, leaving only the heavier ones with soap in them to be packed. This idea, from the shop floor, was remarkably simple, and undoubtedly the cheapest and most efficient solution to the problem at hand.

As this example shows, great ideas come from every level of an organization. Yet the responsibility for establishing and nurturing an environment conducive to creative thinking lies with the leader. Innovation is often a messy process, and employees are more likely think out of the box if they feel reassured that some degree of failure is accepted. To kick-start innovation, leaders need to encourage the exchange of ideas, urge people at every level to experiment, and develop a tolerance for mistakes.

Existing research, as well as our own work, has shown that one primary way to foster innovation is by bringing differing perspectives together, thereby making the most of the diversity that naturally exists within an organization.

Creative Hot Spots

How can you foster an environment in which people can experiment and even dare to fail? Lynda Gratton, professor of management practice at London Business School, addresses this question in her work on "Hot Spots."

(*Continued*)

According to Gratton, Hot Spots are situations in which people are working together in exceptionally creative ways, people feel alive and energized, and their ideas and insights combine with others' in a process of synthesis that generates new ideas and innovation. Hot Spots occur most often in environments of cooperative mind-sets, boundary spanning, and an igniting sense of purpose. Hot Spots emerge; they can't be directed or controlled.[16] Enabling Hot Spots, then, is a leadership challenge that can't be ignored. This incubation of ideas can assist in building and sustaining a culture where ideas are embraced and the race to develop new products and reinvent processes and systems are the key elements for growth. This is the case at 3M, Apple, Google, Herman Miller, Infosys, and others. Developing an environment that values creativity and innovation requires proactive leadership, including actions such as:

1. Integrating creativity and innovation into the core values of the enterprise.
2. Allocating time and space for people to experiment, dream, and envision.
3. Creating opportunities for cross-functional teams to challenge current assumptions and explore possibilities.
4. Periodically, scheduling meetings with one agenda item: envision the future.

5. Establishing specific areas in the building where people are encouraged to gather and play.
6. Fostering an environment in which people feel safe to experiment.
7. Inviting inventors to come and spend a day with your employees.
8. Recognizing and rewarding ideas that succeed as well as those that fail.
9. Use key customers as a source of new ideas.
10. Create platforms for learning on which people can present and discuss ideas.

EMBRACING DIFFERENCES IN THINKING: FROM THEORY TO PRACTICE

In the abstract, encouraging creativity sounds easy. Yet how does this translate to a leader's capacity to foster innovation within an organization? To answer this question, let us get back to the leader's primary task: to achieve results. We are all held responsible for results in many parts of our lives, but perhaps nowhere more *explicitly* than in business, where it's a given that senior leaders must focus on the bottom line. Because of this, monthly sales, quarterly earnings, and annual revenue targets are main points of discussion—and of pain. As leaders, we must embrace this focus. After all, if we fail to align ourselves with the organization's priorities, we undermine our ability to succeed.

Rather than challenging this basic reality, the opportunity to innovate lies in creative execution. Are there better ways to achieve sustainable performance? Do we understand our customers' changing needs? Are we aware of the new competitive landscape? Asking these questions and continuously seeking to answer them take place in the fertile domain of creative thinking. Within an organization, the best way a leader can access a wide array of perspectives is to encourage diversity in the ways that team members both think about and respond to problems.

The ancient Greeks identified four distinct temperaments—sanguine, melancholic, choleric, and phlegmatic—and postulated that our basic temperament affects every aspect of our lives. Later, seminal psychologists like Carl Jung and Abraham Maslow extended the field of study to personality types and psychological stages. The Myers-Briggs Type Indicator, developed in the 1940s and still in wide use today, is a direct descendent of Jung's personality types theory. Similar tools and assessments, including Katherine Benziger's Benziger Thinking Styles Assessment (BTSA) and David Keirsey's Temperament Sorter Model, have been developed in this vein.

In the area of cognitive development, Benjamin Bloom's Taxonomy of Learning Domains and Howard Gardner's theory of Multiple Intelligences, both influential during the last forty years, examine the question of how and why we think the way we do—each through a unique lens. Dan Goleman has postulated that emotional intelligence, more than any other competence, is key to unlocking superior performance, in ourselves and in others. Yet we know that we need to develop both EQ and IQ in order to innovate.

Other incarnations of this line of inquiry, many of which are particularly relevant to the business setting, have centered on neurological function. According to these theories, each individual, through a unique blending of genetic and environmental inputs, develops habitual ways of perceiving and responding to situations. According to Gregory Berns, "The brain takes shortcuts in the interest of efficiency. This means that it will draw from past experiences and any other source of information, such as what other people say, to make sense of what it is seeing . . . It works so well we are hardly ever aware of this process."[17] The upshot of this efficiency is that we default to conventional thinking. Berns goes on to note that in order to unleash innovation, we must rewire our thinking and free up our responses, through such practices as creating analogies, asking questions, seeking novelty, and identifying and associating weak signals in our environment.[18]

In addition, as mentioned previously, integrative thinking, introduced by Roger Martin in his book *The Opposable Mind*, refers to the brain's ability to hold two opposing ideas in constructive tension and "creatively resolve the tension between [the] two ideas by generating a new one that contains elements of the others but is superior to both."[19] Integrative thinking comes about by exploring seemingly unrelated areas of inquiry and continuously posing "what if" scenarios—bringing to mind Apple's iconic challenge to "think different."

What all of this tells us is that innovation can be cultivated. As individuals, we can work at thinking creatively.
However, leaders need to support that effort. Organizations
cannot afford to make costly mistakes that are, in large part,
failures of imagination. Successful companies are those that
reinvent themselves before their competitors do. As such, they
realize that people are their greatest asset. In order to strengthen
that human capital, they must understand and foster their
people's ability to imagine and invent.

Jerry Rhodes, Head of Education & Training Rank Xerox,
has done significant work on thinking in organizations. As the
founder of Effective Intelligence and someone we have worked
with extensively, Rhodes, along with Sue Thame, designed the
Thinking-Intentions Profile called Rhodes's TIP, which color-
frames three main categories of thinking preferences.[20] We
have used this tool to encourage leaders to be more effective
by understanding cognitive preferences and leveraging the
natural diversity of teams.

These basic categories are further refined into hard and
soft sub-groupings, where hard colors connote more objective,
tangible, and logical tendencies; and soft colors suggest more
subjectivity. All are based on the *Thinking-Intentions* discovered
by Rhodes's research with international businesses. The following are examples of how these thinking preferences may present
themselves in the decision-making process.

The first thinking preference, known as the "blue" mind-
set, characterizes thinking that is driven by *what is right*. The
second, called the "red" mind-set, demonstrates a preference

for *finding the truth*. The third thinking preference, called the "green" mind-set, shows a penchant for *seeking the new*. These basic categories are further refined into hard and soft subgroupings, wherein *hard* colors connote more objectivity, tangible, and logical tendencies, and *soft* colors suggest more subjectivity. The following are examples of how these thinking preferences may present themselves in the decision-making process.

○ **Blue Thinking**: Blue thinkers want to make decisions quickly. They tend to be impatient and are motivated by their logic and passion. They size up a situation and are driven by a need for closure. They use their past experience as their guide, and they trust their gut. Blue thinkers believe they know what is right and wrong. The greatest contribution of the blue thinking preference is swift and decisive action, but these thinkers may be at risk of rushing to judgment.

Hard blue thinkers use objective criteria, such as weighted averages, to make quick decisions. They are rational. They look at the advantages and disadvantages of an idea and focus on pros and cons. Logic rules hard blue. *Soft blue* thinkers use subjective criteria and make decisions based on values. They listen to their gut and act because they believe it is the right thing to do. Both hard and soft blue come to a decision because it is affirming. Their passion to excel at times induces them to cut corners and find loopholes in policies and norms.

○ **Red Thinking**: Red thinkers are propelled by the need for voluminous facts and data. They are evidence-based. Their greatest contribution is leaving no stone unturned. Hard red thinkers might come across as conservative and risk averse.

They tend to ask many questions in search of the truth. *Hard red* thinkers use quantitative data. They are analytic and tend to be driven by numbers and spreadsheets. They use data to look for insight into their business environment. *Soft red* thinkers use subjective evidence. Instead of focusing on facts, they seek interaction with others. They are more experiential and impressionistic. Compared to hard red thinkers, soft reds use a more qualitative approach to finding the truth. Their inclination allows them to rely on their observation, impressions, and interactions with others (see sidebar).

In the Red

An investment team we worked with was buying up businesses in Japan, China, and Korea and combining them in one holding company for resale. The benefit of the consolidation process, they determined, was that it would remove 20 percent of the total cost structure for each company, netting them a bundle. They did careful quantitative analysis and crunched the numbers before choosing companies. But the due diligence team failed to talk directly to customers. It turns out that the Korean market is very different from those in Japan and China. The combined companies failed in Korea because no one did the soft red thinking, which revolves around interaction and communication. As a result, they were unable to achieve the 20 percent cost reduction their business model called for.

○ **Green**: Green thinkers are innovators. They tend to rely on the future as opposed to the past or present. Their minds constantly generate ideas, solutions, and options in order to remove barriers and improve operations. *Hard green* thinkers are more focused on evolutionary changes. They are constantly thinking about ways to improve processes and streamline systems. Continuous improvement is their key preference. Hard green thinkers can overwhelm the organization with the sheer quantity of their ideas. *Soft green* thinkers are focused on revolutionary changes. They are visionaries. For soft greens, incremental improvement is an enemy of change. For them there is no "box." Their minds are on a bigger and more compelling future. They go to places where no one else dares to go, and thus they revolutionize industries, organizations, and countries.

INTEGRATING CREATIVE INSIGHT WITH DATA AND ANALYSIS

Many organizations have adopted the Thinking Intensions Profile work of Rhodes and Tham to integrate creative insight with data and analysis. In our work, we have used it with companies in order to encourage holistic thinking and collaboration. To test the framework, we conducted numerous experiments in which we grouped red, green, and blue thinking individuals according to type and gave them an hour to solve a problem. The results were striking. The red groups took their time, conducted a thorough analysis of the task, and came back with one well-supported strategic idea. In contrast, the blue groups were fast and decisive, submitting their recommendations in a relatively short period of time, always with authority and self-assurance. And the green teams produced dozens of big ideas—they were prolific and armed with options and scenarios. However, time and again we've seen that, by far, the most interesting and innovative ideas emerge when we create heterogeneous teams.

Ultimately, good decision making comes about when a leader can leverage thinking from all six of the thinking preferences. The quality of organizational thinking improves as each of the thinking preferences is integrated into the team. The key is in setting certain ground rules. First, each individual on the team should understand the relative strengths and shortcomings of her own thinking preferences. Second, all team members must understand and respect the general orientation of the other thinking preferences. Finally, the leader needs to reinforce the idea that all thinking preferences are valid and useful in generating powerful, actionable, and sustainable solutions.

The benefit of this type of model lies in the capacity to leverage the intrinsic talent of diverse individuals to accomplish a shared goal. Managed carefully, every member of the group is valued for, and takes pride in, his unique contribution. In addition, the whole outcome is invariably greater than the sum of the individual parts. Regardless of what model you use, engineering diversity to drive creative thinking fosters an environment in which disparate ideas can be associated. This is the fertile ground of creative thinking—and it can be effectively applied not only to decision making but also to planning, negotiation, team management, conflict resolution, and change management. In all these domains, better thinking leads to better results.

This approach is particularly effective in meetings. As anyone with organizational experience knows only too well, meetings are often conducted with limited concrete outcomes. This perennial inefficiency stems from the fact that some of the attendees (blue thinkers) like to make quick decisions, whereas others (reds) like to get their ducks in a row, asking many questions before they can reach an agreement. Then, when the green thinkers on the team enter the fray, they confound the rest by continuing to surface more and more ideas and scenarios. This creates what we call the *clash of mind frames*, and can result in a heightened level of stress and anxiety.

To remedy this, we encourage meeting participants to follow a simple set of procedures. In essence, it is a sequence that includes and validates all of the thinking types. First, we encourage blue team members to start by stating the purpose of the meeting. After that, the focus moves to addressing the root causes of the problems, whereby red thinkers candidly acknowledge the reality of the situation and present the available evidence. From the analytical stage we encourage the green team to lead the process and to think out of the box to come up with scenarios and possible solutions. Given that each stage in the process is especially suited for one of the three thinking types, people build on each other's ideas without becoming mired in a rigid approach or succumbing to the insidious power of groupthink. As a team, they can break through barriers that, under normal circumstances, would remain unchallenged. Then, equipped with many new ideas, the team is free to assess and select the most promising approaches. Finally, an action plan is proposed—and a commitment from all team members to execute the plan rounds out the process. This collaborative approach, when successfully implemented, is a powerful way to generate productive ideas and translate them into reality.

In regard to fostering creative thinking, organizations today suffer less from a lack of talent and imagination than from a lack of synergy. Models such as the one just detailed provide a frame to allow individuals to collaborate in a way that captures both creativity and analytical rigor. The most brilliant individual contributions cannot bring real value unless people can connect the dots to full-blown outcomes. To enable this, as a leader you must demonstrate, through your words and deeds, that you value innovation and will commit resources to it. This pillar of creativity is one that can support an organization at every level—in business strategy, product and service development, process management, and customer relations. In addition, an open culture that values and celebrates creativity helps ensure that people are fulfilled and fully engaged. Integrating innovation and creativity into the core values of the organization, and rewarding people for their ideas, are powerful motivators that result in high levels of job satisfaction and a more vibrant culture. This virtuous cycle produces energy, excitement—and business results. There's little doubt that leaders committed to developing and nurturing a culture of innovation position themselves to succeed.

Five Guiding Principles for Fostering Creativity and Innovation:

1. Create a safe environment for people to take risks.
2. Encourage ideas from people at all levels.
3. Focus in on the very best new ideas, and put people together in teams to execute.
4. Schedule activities that foster creativity and encourage innovation.
5. Celebrate small victories and continue to build confidence.

7

The Pillar of Coaching

I have learned that people will forget what you said; people will forget what you did; but people will never forget how you made them feel.

—Maya Angelou

Coaching unquestionably requires focused effort and dedication, but the rewards can be enormous. Bob Nardelli, the former CEO of Home Depot, believes that without a coach, people "will never reach their maximum capabilities."[1] In addition, a recent study out of Stanford demonstrates that formal coaching increases retention rates for students.[2] Given the fact that most business schools lack a sound curriculum in coaching-related skills, more and more companies are picking up the ball and making coaching an integral part of their strategy to develop and grow talent. Coaching sends the signal to employees that an organization cares enough to cultivate their success. And coaching need not be outsourced—leaders can and should develop their own coaching skills.

More and more, CEOs are realizing that their recent recruits, although smart, motivated, and eager to get ahead, lack critical interpersonal skills associated with emotional intelligence—including collaboration, persuasion, and managing conflict. Coaching by leaders helps individuals develop and employ these skills—and vastly improve their performance.

Roger Enrico, the former CEO of PepsiCo, knew this better than anyone. He personally ran a three-day leadership development program for ten senior executives at a time. Enrico did the teaching himself—without any outside consultants. Over the course of the program, the executives developed a "change project" to take back to their respective units. They spent sixty days implementing the project, after which they went back to Enrico for three days of follow-up coaching. Several hundred executives went through the program. All told, the work generated $2 billion in revenue growth and created a strong leadership pipeline.

Later, when Enrico was looking for his successor, a person whom he had watched closely during his training sessions— Steven S. Reinemund—emerged as the obvious choice. Likewise, when Enrico was searching for someone to head Pepsi's restaurant venture, he didn't have to look far to zero in on

David Novak. For his part, Novak went on to use this same leadership development approach all around the world, engaging hundreds of thousands of his staff to make the Yum! Brands restaurants (KFC, Taco Bell, and Pizza Hut, later spun off from PepsiCo) better.[3]

Yet despite the fact that leaders such as Roger Enrico recognize the clear upside of building a coaching pillar, some others still perceive coaching as a purely corrective measure—a last-ditch effort to rein in poor performance. Although it was once used largely to remediate troubled employees, today, in most major organizations, coaching has become an integral part of the standard leadership playbook for elite executives and rising stars. According to *Harvard Business Review*, "Ten years ago, most companies engaged a coach to help fix toxic behavior at the top. Today, most coaching is about developing the capabilities of high-potential performers."[4]

Still, many companies delegate the challenge of coaching to the HR department, thus divesting the manager of any coaching responsibility. One underlying purpose of coaching, however, is to give employees what amounts to a gift—the gift of time. Our research shows that when leaders dedicate time to coaching, the effort is correlated with retention and performance. The leader-as-coach model manifests itself, in many ways, through the concept of "servant leadership" developed by Robert K. Greenleaf, a philosophy and practice by which leaders achieve results for their organizations by giving priority attention to the needs of their colleagues and those they serve.[5] This transforms the role of the leader into that of a mentor and a coach, and as a result, employees develop a sense of belonging—a sense that the organization cares about their well-being and career development.

Beyond retention and personal development, coaching helps people embrace change. As we have seen, organizational change is a complicated endeavor. Human nature causes us to cling to what is familiar and resist what is new and unknown. The first step to change is self-reflection, which is fueled by feedback. The critical role of a coach is to offer that feedback, and to help bring people to a place that they might not reach on their own.

As a leadership tool, coaching is effective at every level of the organization. And its effectiveness goes far beyond a targeted intervention for underachievers or an enrichment program for high performers. Coaching should be an essential competency of every leader. For a coaching mind-set to take root within an organization, senior leaders need to communicate that coaching is the responsibility of every single manager from the top down. It is not a role that should be delegated to a subordinate, a consultant, or the human resources department. Leaders know that coaching is a critical responsibility that they themselves must own.

Coaches are driven by a deep conviction that they can help others to be their best. As advocates for change, they are focused on both the process and the outcome of coaching. To be an effective coach, you need to be aware of your own temperament, propensity toward conflicts, and the motivation underlying the desire to change others. The deeper you dig, the greater the chance you will begin to see yourself realistically. If you avoid dealing with your feelings, or if you don't know your own trigger points, doubt and resentment may rise to the surface at the wrong moment. The bottom line is that you need to know your shortcomings and modulate your own behavior before you can elicit the best from the people around you.

Beyond self-awareness, building a coaching pillar requires agility. Leaders need to be able to blend hard and soft skills and to balance authority and influence. To engage the minds of the people you coach, you must alternately probe and listen, provide honest feedback, and approach difficult conversations with grace and patience. You need to walk the line between being firm and being supportive, listening and directing, focusing on tasks and being sensitive to the emotional needs of others. In addition, to build a coaching pillar, a leader must be driven by an inner belief that people can change. Coaching is an upbeat, glass-half-full endeavor that requires you to find the best in others.

CHALLENGES INHERENT IN COACHING

Alana, the founder of a service-based company in the Northeast, was accustomed to high achievement. Extremely driven, her pace was considered a sprint, and she built a successful career in management consulting at a relatively young age. With an idea that she picked up from colleagues in financial services, and financing from private investors, she started a company and grew it over time to $100 million in revenues through sheer force of will. But soon after that, revenue hit a wall and she and her management team found it difficult to break through certain barriers to growth. Alana's behavior during that time called her leadership skills into question, and morale around the company became a problem.

It did not take long to see that Alana herself was the biggest problem. Although she was brilliant at driving the business, her leadership style was abrasive and abusive. Her staff suffered from a sort of corporate Stockholm syndrome, having invested too much time and energy to leave, but nonetheless feeling entirely exhausted and demoralized. They needed clear direction and a sense of how their work fit into the overall mission of the company. They also needed a less volatile CEO. Unfortunately, the longer sales remained stalled, the more Alana acted out. She blocked any and all attempts to modify her behavior; in fact, she fired those who were willing to give her honest feedback. She was advised many times to get coaching, but she steadfastly refused.

In time, Alana brought in a few seasoned managers to fill the gaps, after which her investors managed to convince her to step away from day-to-day operations and focus on strategic planning and business development. The most significant effect of this shift was that she was no longer in charge of managing people.

Over the next several years she focused on the strategic side of the business and developed a compelling growth strategy. The leadership team managed the people side of the enterprise. It was a successful formula and the business began to grow again. With projections on the upswing, the leadership team created a positive and productive environment that was attracting talent. Over the next several years the company grew revenues to over $500 million. The rapid success drew the attention of other investors and a number of attractive offers began to roll in. Alana, however, could not relinquish control, and she shifted gears again to reclaim a day-to-day leadership role.

Unfortunately, Alana's high IQ and past achievements were not sufficient to equip her to lead, and most of the young people who had joined the company became disillusioned. Performance suffered and the company's fortunes changed significantly. The great tragedy was that she never came to terms with her role in the company's decline and was therefore unable to change her behavior and live up to her full potential.

Alana's disdain of coaching is not unique. Very often abrasive executives perceive being coached as a stigma. Their strong egos make them oblivious to their surroundings and deprive them of the opportunity to learn and lead more effectively.

If Alana had been open to receiving feedback things could have been different. She might have turned herself and her company around. But coaching takes a leap of faith. It forces individuals to explore their weaknesses and expose their vulnerabilities. In the same way that senior executives and CEOs benefit from outside coaching, so too can individuals in an organization benefit when leaders are able to build this pillar within themselves. Building a coaching pillar helps to improve performance and change behavior. Implemented effectively, coaching can help deliver results. Conversely, when a leader neglects to build a coaching pillar, results suffer. Make no mistake, coaching is one of the most effective skills a leader can have and is a central component of leading with conviction. As a tool to manage and motivate employees, coaching is a key for unlocking personal and organization potential.

Because the ultimate goal of coaching is to change behavior and improve performance, leaders need to be aware of some of the difficulties inherent in the process. The following are some of the challenges we have witnessed that can force coaching efforts off the rails.

Cultural Norms

Coaching requires something that is exceedingly difficult for most of us—an honest dialogue. How many times have you come out of an important conversation feeling uneasy because what you said was not what you really meant? The cost of repeated failures to communicate—in terms of time, productivity, and organizational performance—can be huge. People are typically taught to be polite and courteous. In many cultures negative feedback is perceived as counterproductive. We are told as children that we should avoid embarrassing other people by revealing our thoughts about them. Therefore we grow up believing that avoidance is acceptable behavior. We learn to couch our remarks in a way that avoids putting people on the spot. This behavior becomes habitual, and by the time we get to the workplace it is deeply ingrained.

Many corporate and organizational training programs reinforce these habits by coaching managers to "say something nice" before offering critical feedback. In some eastern cultures this practice is associated with "saving face." Regardless of culture, these norms can create confusion, cloud the truth, and impede dialogue. Therefore an honest dialogue requires a combination of courage and respect. It calls for a clear message that is balanced with the appropriate delivery.

The Desire to Be Liked

Leaders want to be liked, the same as everyone else. Consequently, real coaching generally falls by the wayside in favor of euphemisms and pats on the back. But avoiding difficult conversations rarely fosters effective relationships. In fact, quite the opposite is true. When people fail to meet our expectations, we tend to accumulate negative feelings toward them. When we avoid acknowledging our disappointment, our feelings remain hidden below the surface. If a manager fails to address an issue with an employee, the employee will continue that behavior and assume all is well. Eventually, the manager will be forced to address the issue, but the reaction, having built up over time, may seem exaggerated and emotionally charged. This "cashing out" of negative feelings triggers behaviors that are associated with low emotional intelligence: passive-aggression, anger, and silence.

The same effect applies when a manager fails to live up to an employee's expectation. We encountered a situation recently in which a manager repeatedly cancelled regularly scheduled meetings with a direct report. The employee felt that he could not safely mention how much this behavior frustrated him. His resentment built up over time. Finally, after a fifth cancellation, the employee stormed into his manager's office and angrily threatened to quit. Addressing the issue at the outset would have freed up energy and fostered more productive communication.

The desire to be liked creates miscommunication in the same way that cultural norms cause us to couch our remarks. It is not uncommon, then, to hear employees complain during an exit interview that their manager never shared her views about negative performance. In fact, many individuals are surprised to read the long list of gripes their managers have reported to the HR representatives. A dismissal conversation is the first time they are hearing the feedback.

Lack of Skills

Our research shows that a lack of skill in preparing and conducting coaching sessions is another reason leaders avoid meaningful interactions. When attempting to tell it like it is during a negative assessment, for example, a manager may backpedal. This may stem from either limited experience engaging in challenging conversations or painful memories of a time when a confrontation caused them embarrassment. Regardless, poor skills and low confidence can cause coaching to go hopelessly awry. Managers become defensive and say things they don't mean, leading to hurt feelings and resentment. Trust is broken and misunderstanding prevails. The antidote to skill deficiency—in this case and others—is training. With training and experience, the level of skill and confidence a leader brings to the task of coaching become an asset.

Fear of Unintended Consequences

Concern over negative repercussions can cause us to hold back. The CEO of a Fortune 100 company we work with, for example, became frustrated with his senior VP of human resources for not moving quickly enough to manage certain staffing issues. As a result, their meetings were tense and superficial. The CEO hinted at the problem but was never explicit. The senior VP suspected that his boss was dissatisfied but didn't ask why. Both were reluctant to bring the problem into the open. The CEO was concerned that negative feedback would throw the senior VP further off his game. The senior VP was hesitant to broach the subject for fear that the conversation would result in his dismissal. Rather than approaching the problem honestly and constructively, both executives left the problem unresolved and lived with the uncertainty. Consequently, the CEO didn't get the support he needed from HR, and the senior VP was never an effective member of the executive team. Business suffered, and the board eventually replaced both executives.

Shortage of Time and Energy

Leaders are often fighting fires. Confronted with competing agenda items and time pressure, they can be reluctant to engage in difficult interactions. Challenging situations require preparation and follow-up and can entail reviewing a paper trail. One senior executive at a large finance company admitted that he had no problem calling an employee into his office and expressing dissatisfaction with his performance. What bothered him, however, was realizing that he should have had the conversation much sooner. His schedule slowed him down. Because of his own procrastination, he became anxious, and his delivery was defensive. As a result, he earned a reputation for being rude and difficult.

Avoidance of Intimacy

Honest dialogue has the potential to create intimacy—a situation that makes many leaders uncomfortable. Maintaining a safe distance requires less energy and emotional commitment.

All things considered, avoidance may seem like the best option to a manager. An executive from a leading German firm we work with confirmed that raising prickly issues required a much higher level of engagement than simply "carrying on." He therefore continued to maintain a blissful avoidance of problems while serious issues languished unresolved.

Limited Trust

Coaching, at its essence, requires trust. When a culture is driven by internal competition and clouded with secrecy, it becomes difficult to carry out an honest conversation. In one case, an executive from a large global company realized that he needed coaching but was extremely reluctant for fear that the conversation was secretly being tape recorded. Needless to say, trust is hard to build and easy to destroy. Yet, without trust, effective coaching is impossible.

Although all of these factors make coaching a challenge, establishing an open and honest dialogue is worth the effort.

Benefits of Coaching

Coaching is a process aimed at helping people to get better in performing their roles. The following are the positive outcomes of coaching:

(Continued)

- Maximizes human potential
- Builds skills and confidence
- Enhances commitment to learning
- Improves job satisfaction and development
- Radiates a culture and values of compassion and caring
- Develops a meaningful partnership that results in creativity and innovation
- Prepares individuals for increased responsibilities
- Expands the role of executives from being managers to being teachers and facilitators
- Opens up the organization for an honest dialogue that improves performance
- Accelerates results in terms of customer satisfaction, employee retention, and profitability

PREPARING TO COACH

Effective coaching requires leaders to redefine their role in several different ways.

First, they need to move away from pure authority in favor of interaction. They need to go from being directive to becoming a facilitator. At its essence, coaching is about building a sustainable trust, enabling both parties—the coach and the coachee—to be candid. Once the trust level is established, the coach becomes less concerned with being "politically correct" and more focused on improving performance and managing behaviors.

Next, an effective coach needs to grapple with two apparently contradictory objectives. For starters, they must understand the aspirations of their people: what are their hopes and dreams, as well as their strengths and weaknesses? If an individual aspires to be an IT director in five years, how can you support that goal? But they must also be entirely versed in the goals of the wider organization. The best coaches are committed to the coaching process, yet they are staunchly results-oriented. Every individual's goals should be considered in the context of the organization's needs. This ideal means that in order to help people succeed, leaders must thoroughly understand the goals and landscape of their organization.

In addition, coaching requires an explicit top-down commitment. Leaders must demonstrate a dedication to the process. Jeff Immelt of GE, for example, dedicates almost 50 percent of his time to coaching and interacting with his top executives. He understands that coaching is a partnership aimed at enhancing performance and that it builds self-esteem and mutual respect. In fact, in one of his presentations to Harvard MBA students, he said that if he were to repeat his MBA, he would take fewer courses on marketing and finance and more on how to develop people. GE, more than any other company, has produced the largest number of CEOs from its ranks.[6] It is driven by a culture that rewards managers who are committed to developing their people.

Even beyond an organizational commitment, the wider corporate culture needs to be conducive to coaching efforts in order to make them stick. It's clear that what works in an entrepreneurial culture like Google, for example, won't fly at Philip Morris. Some companies expect people to "think different" and disrupt the status quo, whereas others build their business around process guidelines and protective procedures. Companies like Siemens and GE tend to appreciate individuals who are daring competitors. Companies like DuPont and Sinopec might expect employees to be more process oriented and risk averse. The leader's job is to recognize the behaviors that the organization rewards and build them into each individual's development plan.

Taking organizational culture and values into account as you coach enables you to determine which skills and behaviors to cultivate. There's no point in training managers to be risk takers if they work for a strictly risk-averse organization. Likewise, it makes no sense to develop consensus-building skills in a highly competitive culture where the highest values are speed and execution. Your coaching efforts should match the organizational focus.

Finally, coaching demands good communication. This means the willingness to listen. Warren Bennis calls it being a "charismatic listener." Active listening, of course, entails asking questions. But what differentiates a good coach from the rest is the ability to actively and meaningfully listen to the responses. We have all been trained in effective communication techniques, but the challenge comes in dedicating the time to follow through when your attention is pulled in many different directions. However, the cost of failing to listen actively is, at a minimum, a missed opportunity to have an honest dialogue, and in the worst case, a loss of trust.

A common pitfall for managers is approaching issues with a certain bias and therefore not seeking to understand the other person's perspective. This may be the result of arrogance or rigidity. Either way, it tends to turn the dialogue into a monologue. To ask good questions, a coach must project confidence without arrogance—because good questions demonstrate a personal vulnerability that invites others to share in a similarly open way. Active listening is the centerpiece of an honest dialogue and a centerpiece of coaching. Using a structured approach to get the dialogue started is helpful, as long as you can adjust it to suit your style and situation.

The next section presents a conversation framework that allows leaders to manage a coaching session, remain on track, and create a rhythm in the discussion. Once you get going, a natural dialogue will develop around this framework.

A FRAMEWORK FOR THE COACHING CONVERSATION

We have developed an effective framework that we consistently use as we coach executives from a variety of organizations and across cultures. This model is built on three major components: preparing for the coaching meeting, the meeting itself, and follow-up.

Phase 1: Precoaching Reflection

1. Examine and understand the landscape, the culture, and the demands of the organization.
2. Analyze the individual you are coaching in terms of personality type and his or her strengths and weaknesses.
3. Collect data on the individual, including achievements as well as behaviors and skills that need to be developed.
4. List meaningful questions that need to be asked. Start with the easy and end with more complex questions.
5. In terms of delivering critical feedback, anticipate the individual's reaction and be prepared for defensive behaviors ranging from silence to outbursts of anger and blame.

Phase 2: During the Coaching Interaction

1. Create an environment that is conducive to interaction. Sit next to the individual or at a round table, for example, as opposed to sitting behind the desk. This sends the message that "we are in this together."
2. Open with positive remarks. Share some of your own difficulties from your own experience.
3. Acknowledge the tension in the situation and assure the person of confidentiality and trust.

4. Ask questions that require the individual to dig deeply. Listen closely to both verbal and nonverbal responses.

5. Agree on the issues surfaced and development needs. Remain positive.

6. Explore solutions collectively. Ask for options. Solicit ideas for correcting the behavior under discussion or the skill that needs to be improved.

7. Chart a roadmap and get a commitment for implementation.

Phase 3: Postcoaching

1. Set periodic meetings to measure progress.

2. Praise changes and progress, no matter how small. This is an opportunity to deepen trust and build confidence.

3. Continue to collect data and accumulate observations to be shared and discussed.

The Top Ten Coaching Questions

It is possible to provide a very rewarding coaching session by merely asking a series of questions. The following are the top ten questions that could be used in a Socratic coaching approach.

(Continued)

1. What do you want?
2. Can you elaborate?
3. How do you feel about it?
4. What ideas do you have?
5. What are the lessons?
6. How will you achieve your plan?
7. If it goes wrong, what is your backup plan?
8. How are you going to measure progress?
9. What support do you need?
10. What can I do to help?

THE IMPORTANCE OF LISTENING

Facilitating these kinds of questions requires coaches to be "charismatic listeners." When coaches actively listen they build trust. Listening is one of the most effective influence tools. It radiates a sense of caring and empathy. Furthermore, when the listening is authentic it results in a better attitude, stronger partnership, and greater commitment to the desired outcome. Listening is best depicted in the Chinese character, which symbolizes three required elements (see Figure 7.1). First, we must listen with the ears for verbal messages. Second, we listen with the eyes to observe nonverbal messages. Third, we listen with our hearts to sense the emotions expressed in the message.

Ear  Eye
One (undivided)

Heart

Figure 7.1: The Chinese Character "To Listen"

The Effective Leveling Checklist

In coaching it is critical to conduct an open and honest dialogue. This involves giving people feedback, or what we call leveling. To level is to give honest and straightforward feedback in order to encourage development, build the relationship, or both.

When leveling, you need to be . . .

1. Clear about your objective and the purpose of the feedback
2. Focused on behaviors rather than the person
3. Specific, rather than general
4. Straightforward and not apologetic for the point you are making
5. Aware of timeliness and location
6. Willing to test your assumptions
7. Sensitive to self-esteem issues
8. Sincere, credible, and emotionally controlled

THE COACHING METAPHOR:
A REALITY CHECK

Our mental models for coaching are forged in the sports arena. Yet celebrity coaches are idiosyncratic, and their methods and results vary widely. Vince Lombardi and Phil Jackson are larger-than-life figures with egos to match; Bobby Knight threw chairs and was nicknamed the General; Joe Paterno failed to take a stand when confronted with a situation that tested his morals; and Billy Bean revolutionized baseball economics and became the centerpiece of a bestselling book. In other words, every coach's profile is unique. Sometimes the sporting analogy holds; sometimes it's off the mark. However, if there is one coach who we believe sets an example for coaches on and off the field, it would be John R. Wooden, UCLA's iconic head basketball coach.

Wooden, who passed away on June 4, 2010, at the incredible age of ninety-nine, was nicknamed the Wizard of Westwood.[7] In his twenty-seven-year tenure, he coached UCLA to ten NCAA national championships in a twelve-year period (1964–1975), including seven in a row (1967–1973), an unprecedented feat. Within this period, his teams won a record eighty-eight consecutive games. He was named national coach of the year six times, and the Pac-10 Coach of the Year Award in both men's and women's basketball was renamed the John Wooden Coach of the Year Award. While a student and basketball star himself at Purdue University, Wooden was the first player to be named basketball All-American three times. In

1932, he led Purdue to the Helms Foundation's unofficial national championship and was named national player of the year.

Wooden was beloved by his former players, among them Kareem Abdul-Jabbar and Bill Walton. His leadership philosophy was, "Adjust to your players, but don't expect them all to adjust to you. Teamwork is not a preference, it's a necessity. A good leader is first, and foremost, a teacher."[8] To encourage others to reach deeply within themselves, to become better *and* to accept the things that they cannot improve, a leader must become a master of self-awareness. Leaders should reflect on their own actions and consider the reasons for using a particular style of leadership before they actually use it. Wooden did just that. He spent fourteen years observing himself and identifying twenty-five behaviors he believed were necessary to achieve success. In 1948 he summarized this monumental work in his Pyramid of Success.

Wooden's Pyramid of Success is legendary. In it he identifies fifteen essential building-block behaviors—including industriousness, alertness, and poise—which are held together by underlying traits such as faith and patience. To Wooden, coaching was about gaining and showing mutual esteem, respect, loyalty, and devotion. He did not create the Pyramid to dictate his beliefs, but rather to live by them himself. Through great introspection, adaptability, and the mastery of emotions, he developed both self-discipline and a path to discipline for those under his supervision. As a coach, Wooden was an expert observer. He was quick to spot a weakness and correct it or use it as a teachable moment. He was willing to sacrifice personal considerations for the welfare of all. That defined him as a team player. He never used the word "winning" or exhorted his teams to be "number one," only to be "the best you can become." He believed that successfully developing the building blocks of character ultimately led to competitive greatness.

Abdul-Jabbar recalled in the *New York Times* that with Wooden there "was no ranting and raving, no histrionics or theatrics." He continued: "To lead the way Coach Wooden led takes a tremendous amount of faith. He was almost mystical in his approach, yet that approach only strengthened our confidence. Coach Wooden enjoyed winning, but he did not put winning above everything. He was more concerned that we became successful as human beings, that we earned our degrees, that we learned to make the right choices as adults and as parents."

"In essence," Abdul-Jabbar concluded, "he was preparing us for life."[9]

These are essential lessons for leaders—as coaches and as individuals. In the organizational setting, the leader as coach must be consistent, thoughtful, and grounded in the organization's reality. Leaders who coach need to ask good questions and demonstrate patience. They need to exhibit empathy and provide honest feedback. Coaches need to encourage two-way dialogue and also obtain a commitment for change. To manage this, you must first cultivate these traits within yourself and then practice coaching others toward greatness.

Five Guiding Principles for Building a Pillar of Coaching:

1. Leaders must make coaching an organizational priority, beginning from the top down.
2. Every leader should develop the skills needed to coach.
3. Coaching should not be delegated to the HR department.
4. Effective coaching requires the ability to level; that is, to engage in open and honest feedback.
5. Coaches must ask good questions and actively listen to produce positive outcomes.

8

The Pillar of Collaboration

Alone we can do so little; together we can do so much.

—Helen Keller

Collaborating in self-managed teams is a complex but rewarding goal, particularly for global companies with a multitude of overlapping and interdependent operations spanning the landscape. This proved true for the venerable producer of paper and wood products Champion International in the late 1980s after industry veteran Richard E. Olsen took on the challenge of making the company more efficient following their merger with the St. Regis Corporation.

Established in 1883, Champion was a family-owned business until 1960. After the St. Regis merger, Champion became a leader in several prominent segments of the paper market and one of the largest private landowners in the United States. Although widely respected, the company was vulnerable to takeover attempts because of the new size and scope of its business.[1]

Olsen, in full partnership with chairman and CEO Andrew C. Sigler, was committed to the organization's employees and determined to find ways to improve operations and efficiently redesign the work through teams. From Bucksport, Maine, to Canton, North Carolina, Champion's mills were restructured to rely more on decentralized decision making and less on traditional management.

Transforming managers into change agents and inspiring machine operators and union members to become collaborative was revolutionary in the mid-1980s. The restructuring involved the creation of teams, whose responsibilities ranged from hiring to operational decisions to shutting down product lines if quality was questioned by any of the operators. Teams were responsible for all aspects of the operation, from inventory to shipment. They even opted to be paid for a four-day workweek instead of calling for layoffs when demand was down due to cyclicality in the industry.

As a result of the bold shift to self-managed teams, safety improved, product quality increased, and morale was at an all-time high. In 1996, Olsen, then a twenty-nine-year Champion veteran, was elevated to chairman and CEO. Although Champion International was eventually acquired by International Paper, making the new company the largest in the world,

Olsen left a legacy of commitment and innovation that is evidenced today in the paper industry.

High-functioning teams can have an exponential (positive or negative) impact on the results of a company. In their book *Multipliers*, Liz Wiseman and Greg McKeown suggest that leaders can amplify the capabilities of individuals operating in teams. Multipliers, they say, maximize the collective brainpower within their organizations, in part by leveraging teams.[2] However, according to Harvard professor J. Richard Hackman, a leading authority on the subject, a team is only as effective as the environment in which it operates. Not surprisingly, Hackman says that a supportive organizational context, with leaders that fully utilize each individual's talents, makes every difference to the success of a team.[3]

Effectively cultivated, teams serve to raise morale and engage each individual's sense of purpose and accomplishment. As Benjamin Franklin said, *We must all hang together, or assuredly we shall all hang separately*. It is a symbiotic relationship: teams become stronger thanks to a good leader, and good leaders become better with the help of a strong team. Like an expert conductor, leaders who can get everyone reading from the same sheet of music, and performing together in harmony despite differences, can tap into all of the advantages that teams bring to the party.

Creating and leading teams that are equipped to collaborate is one of the most critical, and challenging, pursuits of leadership. It is a sign of the times that the Bruce Willis archetype (and the John Wayne archetype before him)—the righteous hero acting alone to get the job done—is a thing of the past. The environment in which we live and work is far too complex to accomplish anything important alone. Unfortunately, insecurity and lack of courage are just two reasons leaders decide against team empowerment.

We watched a common scenario play out at a luxury manufacturing and distribution company based in the western United States. Founded as a partnership of three college friends, each partner in the firm assumed a principal role in the organization. In the start-up phase, the CEO had oversight of product development and marketing. The second partner, the CFO, was busy with capital acquisition and business model needs. Meanwhile, the third partner managed operations as COO. In the first several years, with the company almost entirely focused on the marketing and finance functions, things proceeded according to plan. However, when that balance shifted to operations, some leadership issues came to light. With manufacturing and distribution suddenly more relevant, the COO's team quickly grew large, and the bulk of the organization became his direct reports. Unfortunately, he lacked experience and self-confidence. As a result, he did not want anyone to witness the mistakes and missteps he and his team were making, so he operated in secret. In fact, he managed the team with a black box model. Yet, given the relatively small size of the business and the speed with which they needed to operate, cross-functional cooperation was mandatory. But it did not happen. Because the COO required stealth from his team, they took his cue and operated apart from the rest of the organization. As a result, no one outside of operations knew what was going on in shipping or within the supply chain. The lines of communication were closed, and the other senior managers were left in the dark. The company quickly became dysfunctional, and it took them years to regain their momentum.

THREE REASONS FOR TEAMS

No matter how smart you are—as a leader or an individual contributor—you can't generate results by yourself. According to Jon Katzenbach and Douglas Smith in their seminal work, *The Wisdom of Teams*, the opportunity for increased performance through teams is too great to let doubt or false assumption cloud your thinking; teams are the path to unlocking performance.[4] Although their book was published over twenty years ago, the conclusions are perhaps even more relevant today than when they were first written. There are three realities that form the rationale for teams today: complexity, collaboration, and efficiency.

1. Complexity

Organizations operate within the wider world—a world in which political changes, economic developments, and remarkable technological advances all crisscross and overlap to create an environment of constant upheaval and opportunity.

New industry competitors emerge overnight. Market conditions and the twenty-four-hour news cycles affect supply and demand. Demographic trends mean that values and needs are forever in flux.

In addition, on top of increasing clock speed and global complexity, mergers and the consolidation of industries complicate the need for high-functioning team dynamics. As multinational firms expand through acquisition, and reporting structures become ambiguous, there is more complexity than ever in team dynamics.

The CEO of a large multinational subsidiary specializing in electronic security products told us about a problem that arose on his senior management team as a result of this complexity. His CFO had a dual reporting relationship: to him and to the CFO of the parent company. The CFO struggled with the reporting alignment and ended up throwing his loyalties to the parent company, to the detriment of that key subsidiary. His perception of the situation was that his career would be better served if his loyalties were clearly aligned with the parent company. Unfortunately, the CFO did not understand the nature of his job and his need to manage the dual reporting relationship well. He was let go from his position and could not find one in the parent company or any of the other subsidiaries. He had been marked as not being a team player, so none of the other operations was willing to accept him.

All of this points to the increased need for effective teamwork and collaborative decision making. As different cultures in opposing time zones become accustomed to working together, many differing mind-sets, experiences, and cultures come together. Creating diverse teams allows us to bring a wider array of ideas and approaches to the table. It allows us to benefit from our differences by creating a more integrated approach.

2. Collaboration

Working collectively, teams can collaborate across disciplines and distances to solve pressing problems. Teams enable individuals to share knowledge and achieve consensus. Although some definitions of collaboration do not include a leadership component at all—instead stressing a model of decentralization—we believe that the leader's job is to support and enable collaboration. In fact, even within self-directed teams informal leaders often emerge. According to Morten Hansen, a management professor at the University of California, Berkeley, and at INSEAD in France, a main challenge leaders must face is to find ways to unify groups so they can work together. In his book, entitled *Collaboration*, he says, "The idea of disciplined collaboration can be summed up in one phrase: the leadership practice of properly assessing when to collaborate (and when not to) and instilling in people both the willingness and the ability to collaborate when required."[5] Hansen goes on to say: "In complex organizational activities, effective collaboration is often a necessary requirement for success."

To be sure, collaboration fuels innovation. In his book *The Difference*, Scott Page, professor of complex systems, political science, and economics at the University of Michigan, concludes that progress depends less on highly trained experts working alone and more on people working together in groups capitalizing on their individual strengths.[6] In addition, a CEO study conducted by IBM found that more than three quarters of the 765 chief executive officers queried cited collaboration and partnering as very important to their innovation efforts.[7]

The takeaway of collaboration is that it leverages collective knowledge, from across industries or across the globe, to make everyone smarter. Teams that collaborate allow best practices, diverse experiences, and lessons learned to filter across the entire group. This has been the experience, and the lifelong mission, of Freeman A. Hrabowski III—the accomplished and influential president of the University of Maryland Baltimore County (UMBC) who is recognized as one of the most influential leaders in education. Hrabowski's trailblazing work in educating minority students in the sciences has elevated UMBC to the national stage.

Hrabowski's dream is to dramatically increase the number of minority math and science majors at UMBC and begin to eliminate the race and gender gaps in technical fields. And he is succeeding. In his thirteen years as president, Hrabowski has steered the university to become a national leader in undergraduate science and engineering. In addition, UMBC is a leading producer of African Americans going on to earn doctorates in these same fields.

How does he do it? By putting students into teams and allowing them to collaborate. As part of the Meyerhoff Scholars Program at UMBC, students are encouraged to work in groups, and they are coached to solve complex problems collectively, as teams of scientists do. To catalyze learning and enhance their interest in science, students work in four-person groups, each with a specific role: manager, researcher, scribe, or blogger. This focus on collaboration over competition has paid off. A National Science Foundation report reveals that forty-eight African Americans who earned bachelor's degrees from UMBC went on to earn doctorates in science and engineering from 2005 to 2009, the largest number from any college without a black student majority.

It is Hrabowski's leadership, and his advocacy of collaboration, that has made this happen. As important as technology-enabled collaboration is, Hrabowski's work illustrates that it is leaders who steer work teams to realize results that would otherwise be impossible to achieve.

3. Efficiency

When teams are working well, it can almost seem like magic: the collective wisdom can exceed the sum of its parts. Great teams are efficient and nimble; they are as innovative as they are focused and reliable. However, in the end it is not magic that makes it work; it is leadership. The best leaders realize that individuals in today's workforce are looking for opportunities to express themselves, and they are eager to contribute in ways that affect results. Leaders can tap into this desire to have an impact through teams. Continuous improvement, after all, is best activated when problems and gaps are addressed through a team approach. Work teams create excitement and transform the workplace into an environment in which people are engaged and constantly searching for a better way.

One of the most interesting examples of team-fostered efficiency is demonstrated by Combat Support Hospitals (CSH). Their mission, as the name implies, is mobility and effectiveness. This translates into being ready to mobilize quickly to create the needed structure and offer medical care in urgent situations. Each member of the team is trained not only to perform his or her role quickly but also to exhibit competence in multiple roles. Some of the elements that characterize these unique teams are a deep commitment to their mission, seamless collaboration, interdependency, and a high level of trust and transparency.

Like a CSH unit, organizations are expected to be increasingly efficient and responsive. By leveraging the power of teams, leaders can solve problems quickly. It is the diversity of skills in teams that delivers innovative results faster to satisfy sophisticated customers demanding an immediate response. In addition, diverse teams are efficient because they integrate silos and approach problems from a wide array of perspectives.

It Takes Courage to Collaborate

Matrixed organizations with complex team dynamics are common today. People have dual reporting relationships, and their teams span time zones and continents. The question for leaders then becomes, *How big is my team?* The question for team members becomes, *To whom do I report?* With these challenges in mind, we created a leadership development exercise.

First, we divide people up into separate tables, asking each to choose a team leader. The leaders come into the hall with us, and we hand out an assignment: They need to put a simple LEGO set together—while their teams are blindfolded. The leaders are sent back to their teams to complete the assignment. Back at the tables, with everyone blindfolded, some leaders realize that they don't have all of the pieces they need to complete the assignment. What do they do? In the end, the exercise is about leaders checking their egos at the door and finding ways to solve a complex problem. Can they find a way to work with the other tables to get the pieces they need? Do they collaborate or are they in competition? Are they open to feedback and ideas from their team or the other leaders at the other tables? The leaders who are open to creative ideas and feedback, and who understand that they can be successful only if they collaborate with the other leaders, fare best.

TEAM FUNCTIONS AND DYSFUNCTIONS

In an article in the *Harvard Business Review* in 2007 titled "The Myth of the Top Management Team," Jon R. Katzenbach, a consultant with McKinsey & Company, argued that groups of top managers working in teams seldom actually worked together in pursuit of a common goal.[8] Our experience tells us that this is often the case throughout organizations—at all levels. Although there are many reasons that teams become dysfunctional, the primary cause we have found is the lack of a shared vision. This failure to communicate goals is a common leadership shortcoming. When leaders don't explain the rationale behind a team, members consider the group to be at best discretionary and at worst a waste of time. As with any business endeavor, individuals want to contribute and succeed—that can't happen unless they are clear on the parameters of the mission.

Also topping our list of why teams fail is a lack of buy-in—from individuals *and* organizations. Many of us are raised as children to be competitive, to strive to excel. For us, the idea of collaboration is not as ingrained as is individual achievement. Therefore when we arrive in the workforce we understand the need for collaboration cognitively, but not emotionally. That lack of conviction causes teams to fizzle out when members lose their initial sense of urgency. Likewise, organizational ambivalence toward team accomplishments stifles their momentum. Organizations often reward superstar individual contributors over exceptional team performance. Again, this points to a leadership imperative. It is the leader's job to bind team performance to individual goals and even to individual compensation. Team output must be a clear priority that maps with organizational objectives, or the group is likely to lose interest.

Poorly defined roles are yet another source of team apathy. When individuals are unclear on their functions and responsibilities, the confusion leads to overlap as well as interpersonal conflicts. As a result, accountability falls by the wayside. Closing the loop on these process points is a prerequisite if people are to work together efficiently. Ground rules need to be stated and understood up front. Likewise, roles within the team need to be made transparent when the team first comes together.

Building effective teams is as difficult a task as any—in part because fear of conflict can sabotage results. When individuals are unable or unwilling to engage in honest dialogue, teams lose their power to earnestly grapple with important issues and they make decisions based on single perspectives. In addition, when team members are unable to express their opinions freely or feel stymied by politics, they fade into the background and lose interest. The result is steamrolling on one end of the spectrum and a lack of consensus on the other.

To paraphrase Harry S. Truman, it is amazing what can be accomplished when nobody cares who gets the credit. But when the opposite it true, teams die a slow death. In their own manner, each of these team killers leads to the same result: an absence of trust. Without trust, team dynamics quickly

Table 8.1: What Does Your Team Look Like?

Low-Trust Team Behaviors	High-Trust Team Behaviors
Negative leadership	Positive leadership
Assigned leadership	Facilitative leadership
Lack of initiative	High frequency of initiative
Low energy	Radiating energy
Limited feedback	Ongoing feedback
Lack of follow-through	Timely responses
Limited exchange of information	Constant information sharing
Blaming behaviors	Praising behaviors
Poor execution skills	Superb execution skills
Carelessness and independence	Thoughtfulness and interdependency

become dysfunctional. The result is blame games and grabbing credit, instead of benefitting from the natural give-and-take flow of an efficiently functional team. Table 8.1 depicts the differences between teams that have a high level of trust and those that do not.

FIVE FUNDAMENTALS OF TEAMS

All too often teams are created with great intentions but are then left to wither, lacking clear guidelines or guidance. Although it has become more and more necessary for people to come together quickly and organically to solve problems on their own, total sovereignty is ineffective in formal work teams. In fact, just a little planning and oversight goes a long way toward keeping teams focused and empowered. To align teams with organizational objectives and avoid potential malfunctioning, we often propose considering the five fundamental elements of teams: relationships, goals, roles, structure, and oversight.

1. Relationship Building

The best teams are made up of individuals with diverse experience and unique strengths. Although that mix can create a foundation for creativity, the formula also comes with inherent challenges. In fact, any team—diverse or not—entails relationship management. As a leader, your job is to surface and manage the interpersonal issues that help or hinder the team's progress. Without attention to interpersonal dynamics, teams become distracted by relationship issues and can fail to meet their basic objectives.

Begin by managing the emotional side of teams. Find ways for the people in the group to get to know each other and explore common interests. This aspect of team leadership may seem time-consuming in the short term, but it will help you sustain the team over the long term. Managing relationships in a team is similar to coaching: It requires validating individual contributions, protecting members from political maneuvering, reminding people about the team's mission and values, challenging the team to succeed, and creating ways to release stress and tension.

Managing interpersonal dynamics also requires leaders to become attuned to a team's particular culture. This is especially relevant when a merger or acquisition brings unlike teams together, as was the case when an engineering solutions company, Aricent, merged with a creative branding company called Frog. Together, the two companies formed a full-service software development firm, bringing both engineering and creative design services to the table for clients. Frog, for its part, was highly creative and innovative, whereas Aricent had a deep expertise in managing complex processes. Although the merger was a sound strategic move, leveraging the strength of both organizations proved to be a challenge because their cultures and values were so different. In this case, as well as others, the hard metrics of finance, marketing, and process are often analyzed before a merger is finalized, but the cultural fit and relationship issues are taken for granted.

The people side of any team endeavor can be complex and unpredictable, even for those among us who are masters at relationship management.

David Gergen, political consultant and advisor to four U.S. presidents, is someone who has a natural ability to deftly manage a complex set of relationships while also reaching the ambitious goals he sets out to achieve. When Gergen came to teach at Harvard University in 1999, he instantly recognized a pressing need for a center dedicated to leadership development. This was something Ronald Heifetz had been working toward at the institution, and when Gergen came aboard he agreed to join the effort. As a journalist, public servant, and educator, Gergen had witnessed firsthand the importance of leadership training—especially at an institution of higher learning (such as Harvard) where students are groomed for future opportunities to lead on the world stage. However, navigating the nuanced web of relationships required building bridges between key stakeholders on different committees and at different schools across the Harvard community. Gergen, who went on to partner with Heifetz to launch the project, was careful to respect the institution's culture and personalities. Rather than charging forward, he used an incremental approach, inviting students and faculty to collaborate and to test different ideas. As codirector in the first year, he worked with Heifetz to solicit support and built a coalition at Harvard to develop the Center for Public Leadership and bring it to life. His accessible demeanor, as well as the positive way he invites feedback and drives change, have earned him a reputation as a true and humble collaborative leader. Today the Center for Public Leadership is one of the most active centers at Harvard and a model for many other institutions. In addition, Gergen's successful attempts to build bridges to the other departments and schools have yielded numerous benefits and joint efforts.

2. Setting Goals

As we have mentioned, communicating priorities is the only way to set a team up to succeed. It is less obvious that the overall vision must be established by the team itself. If a vision and goals are imposed on the team, then each member's resolve will dissolve in the face of conflicting priorities. For members to fully buy into the rationale for the team, they must be an integral part of creating the vision, setting goals, and changing the road map.

The role of the leader is to foster inclusion and participation. For example, the leader should set aside time to have team members share aspirations and think big. In doing so, they can picture and describe what they believe the future should look like. When people work together to envision the future, it strengthens bonds within the team. For some leaders it is difficult letting go of the reins long enough to allow teams to set priorities and determine the agenda. Yet full involvement and team consensus ensures that everyone is more committed to results.

3. Defining Roles

In addition to group priorities, leaders should also ensure that team members become clear on individual expectations. This sets the stage for accountability and eliminates overlap among the team members. Take stock of the talents you have on the team and map them with the skills needed to achieve results. As you define roles, align people with what they are good at, rotating roles when that is feasible. Playing to individual strengths in diverse teams builds confidence and encourages participation. In addition, the flip side of managing individual roles is getting the most out of teams by challenging them.

Inasmuch as you need to cater to diverse strengths, positioning people to grow will keep them engaged even longer.

In terms of roles, leaders need to take into account both team members' strengths and their individual development. Leading with conviction requires a balance of both imperatives.

4. Establishing Structure

It is entirely possible to become under- or overreliant on process. Going overboard with team structure impedes innovation; an absence of structure leads to confusion and grandstanding. Instead of imposing a process, the leader's role is to help establish and enforce ground rules around norms and behaviors. This is an important part of eliminating the barriers to success and allowing individuals to contribute their best ideas.

Encouraging candor, for example, is a basic ground rule. According to Douglas Conant, former CEO of Campbell Soup Company, candid and timely conversations are essential to team success. "Once you have talented people operating in a high-trust environment, a spirit of candor is essential to advancing the agenda . . . The path forward for every team is always forged around a series of course corrections based on what is working and what is not working."[9]

Enforcing ground rules for open communication is particularly important when teams are less diverse, because the majority members may shut out minority dissenters. We have seen this happen repeatedly in our coaching workshops and executive training. For example, as part of a leadership development exercise we conducted at Harvard, we divided executives into teams. Individuals in each group were given an eight-foot piece of rope and one simple objective: create a perfect square with the rope as quickly as possible. We watched with interest as one team of six men and one young woman from NASA tried to make their square. Within the first few minutes, the woman had a simple idea for how to complete the task quickly and effectively. An engineer by training, she thought of a way to ensure that each side was the same length with perfectly angled corners. It was a good idea based on sound logic. She repeated the idea several times but was ignored by everyone. Eventually she gave up and they went about executing a series of less expedient ideas that ended them near last place.

There is ample blame to go around when a team ignores the lone dissenter. Groups that operate with guidelines that stipulate open communication and respect for differing opinions tend to fare better.

Beyond candor, team guidelines should include remaining on point, avoiding blame, discouraging political maneuvering, respecting differing opinions, and defining the parameters of confidentiality.

We worked with a firm that specialized in management consulting within the health care and education sectors. Members of the senior management team in this organization were more credentialed than most. Many of the senior leaders had both an MD and a PhD—and some were JDs as well.

Calling them a brainy group is putting it mildly; and their egos were as high as their IQs. Despite that, or perhaps because of it, the team dynamics were completely dysfunctional. In fact, these quick thinkers had a bad habit of talking over one another. Meetings turned into free-for-alls, and the culture of disrespect was hampering key relationships. In this case, we suggested a few simple ground rules for meetings, beginning with the simple idea that each person should be allowed to finish a thought before others could begin talking. Then, if someone felt that individuals were not adhering to the ground rules, all they had to do was raise two fingers in the air and the meeting would halt for a brief process check. This, and a few other points of simple decorum, went a very long way with this group. Ground rules—when they are carefully established and enforced—help create teams in which people are unafraid to present creative ideas and take the risks that solve problems and drive innovations.

5. Providing Oversight

One of the most important drivers of team performance is leadership. Every team needs a leader to keep them focused and positive—as well as to ensure that they are spending time in pursuit of the appropriate objectives.

In terms of how teams operate and perform, it was the American social psychologist Bruce Tuckman who proposed that groups develop according to four stages—forming, storming, norming, and performing. We have found that teams lose some of their original energy and momentum in between the norming and storming stages. We call this eventuality *falling*, because members tend to fall away as they lose interest and lose sight of their original goals. This is a turning point in the lifecycle of a team when you, as the leader, need to inspire participants and demonstrate that they are supported and valued. In addition, you should act to ensure that the team is working in a supportive organization context. In doing so, it is your job to communicate the group's output and keep senior management apprised of team accomplishments.

Throughout life of the team, it is also your role to measure how the team is performing against expectations. Taking stock and exploring performance gaps will enable you to manage issues head-on, before they become disruptive. The following Team Scorecard is a tool we have designed to help you maintain focus and transparency within a team. Members can access the team periodically, with the results posted and discussed. This self-regulation allows the team to work together to identify gaps and develop their strengths. And the transparency circumvents conflicts that, left unattended, can fester and erode trust.

The Team Scorecard: A Self-Assessment

To get an accurate assessment of your team, have the team rate themselves on the following dimensions. You may also rate the team yourself and compare and contrast your assessment with their self-assessment.

	Strongly disagree				Strongly agree
The vision is clear.	1	2	3	4	5
We follow our guiding principles.	1	2	3	4	5
We are committed to the objectives.	1	2	3	4	5
We understand our roles.	1	2	3	4	5
Our discussions are open.	1	2	3	4	5
Conflicts are resolved openly.	1	2	3	4	5
We respect each other.	1	2	3	4	5
Mistakes are used as learning opportunities.	1	2	3	4	5
Efforts are recognized.	1	2	3	4	5
Meetings are focused and productive.	1	2	3	4	5
Problems are identified and addressed.	1	2	3	4	5
The environment is supportive.	1	2	3	4	5
We are a self-directed team.	1	2	3	4	5
We are creative in problem solving.	1	2	3	4	5
This is the best team I have ever experienced.	1	2	3	4	5
We are productive.	1	2	3	4	5
We encourage feedback.	1	2	3	4	5
We leverage diversity.	1	2	3	4	5
We like each other.	1	2	3	4	5
We follow through.	1	2	3	4	5

Add the points to calculate your score.

Total Score: _____

80–100 points = Above average; continue to develop

60–79 points = Average; could use some improvement

20–59 points = Below average; needs considerable improvement

Leaders understand, intuitively and practically, the need for collaboration and team management. Beyond the utility of orchestrating the work of many individuals according to organizational needs, teams offer leaders the opportunity to have a broad impact on group performance and improve the working relationships among people. And collaboration, done right, can exceed every expectation in terms of delivering new ideas and innovative execution. Yet collaboration is difficult for many leaders because it requires relinquishing power and demonstrating trust. That takes considerable courage and self-assurance. Teams, after all, are more visible than individuals, and failure may reflect poorly on you as a leader. However, the opposite is also true. A team of people performing well, taking initiative and delivering results, is exceedingly satisfying and reflects well on the leader. Leading with conviction entails the quest to bring people together to solve problems and address issues in a collaborative way. Leaders need to determine when a team approach is appropriate and take the time and effort to build teams with the potential to deliver results that individuals acting alone could never achieve.

Five Guiding Principles for Building a Pillar of Collaboration

1. The ability to work in teams and collaborate effectively is paramount in today's complex organizations.

2. Leading teams requires wisdom and maturity from a leader in order to overcome doubt and insecurity.

3. Teams will be stronger and more efficient if they are supported by a foundation of trust and mutual respect.

4. Creativity and innovation is one of the positive by-products of a well-functioning team.

5. Knowing when *not* to collaborate is as crucial as deciding when it is the right approach.

9

The Pillar of
Results

*The competitive difference is not deciding what to do, but how to
do it. Execution becomes paramount.*
                    —Larry Bossidy, former CEO of Honeywell

I t was touted as *the* device that would revolutionize
the delivery of education in the developing world.
Founded by Nicholas Negroponte, the former
director of MIT Media Lab, One Laptop Per Child (OLPC)
was designed to supply 150 million laptops to children in the
Third World by the end of 2008. But just three years after its
launch in 2005, OLPC fell woefully short of expectations,
jeopardizing the initial plan. The price projections overshot
initial estimates, the actual development of the software as
well as the laptop took longer than expected, countries that

had promised to procure the laptops in large quantities backed off, and competition became more aggressive. On another level, the product failed to take off as expected because the end users—children in the developing world—refused to use them. The laptop, as it turned out, was better suited for the developed world—it was out of sync with local realities.[1] Negroponte, who has been legitimately heralded as a "digital visionary" and an "indefatigable leader,"[2] had the right intentions and a high level of ambition. What he was unable to do, however, was translate his vision into reality.

Many leaders encounter the same problem as Negroponte. They have the right ideas and the right vision, but when it comes to delivering results, they fail. Yet that's the whole point of leadership—everything that a leader does is intended to drive results. Those of us who have accepted the challenge of leading with conviction, however, do so to make things better. Therefore the results we are after are more than purely financial. For instance, a supervisor may want a team's return on investment to improve, and she also may want the team to feel satisfied with their contribution. Similarly, a philanthropist may intend for his financial assets to close social gaps, and at the same time he may also want the organization that disperses those assets to model his values. A parent may work to raise a child to become an intelligent and compassionate human being, and he may also want to do it in a family environment that is both healthy and happy. Most leaders measure themselves not only by what they have accomplished personally, but also by what their followers have accomplished. The conductor of an orchestra, for example, may be accomplished in music theory, but the result of his output is the music made by others. Likewise, a business executive may understand the financial environment inside and out, yet it is individual employees interacting with customers that create value for the company. As Howard Schultz, chairman and CEO of Starbucks, once said, "I am not in the business of coffee, serving people; I am in the business of people, serving coffee."[3]

So how do leaders drive better results themselves as well as working through others? In our view, there are three things that leaders must do to achieve this goal: define vision and values, follow a roadmap, and remain dedicated.

DEFINE VISION AND VALUES

First and foremost, leaders need to be propelled by a dream and a sense of purpose. This purpose is the source of energy and innovation and in many ways serves as a compass that sets direction. Some of the greatest leaders of the modern age are best known for their vision. John F. Kennedy, Martin Luther King Jr., Susan B. Anthony, and Nelson Mandela are all leaders whose vision inspired people to act. They offered not only an ideal that resonated but also a path that others wanted to follow. Yet too many leaders dismiss the notion of vision and swiftly move toward framing the mission, goals, and objectives. Although such concrete concepts are important elements in any plan or roadmap, they must be driven by a vision. Without vision, the stormy waters we inevitably face in the pursuit of results may distract and derail us. Our vision is our compass, indicating our true north.[4] Such a compass enables us to move forward; to be propelled by purpose and a cause we believe in. On days when we miss our targets and fail to achieve our goals, it is vision which helps us maintain our direction. In many respects, vision is spiritual in nature. It sustains us; it gives us the energy to defy gravity and bypass disappointments. Vision is what inspires us each morning to get up and seize the day. It is the cathedral for the stonecutter. It is a force that compels us to do something meaningful with our lives. A clear and compelling vision helps us articulate the future. It is the culmination of our emotions and desires to change things, and to enlist others to help. Vision has to galvanize us first, and those we seek to influence second. This is the case for nations, organizations, agencies, communities, families, and each of us as individual leaders.

A vision must be supported by a clear and compelling set of values. Vision inspires; values define a set of beliefs that are nonnegotiable. Values dictate the way we conduct ourselves in pursuit of the vision and are guiding principles for all in the organization. They define our priorities, connect us as teams, and encourage us to commit to things that we might otherwise overlook under pressure. They provide some boundaries for what we can and can't do. Our experience shows that organizations without clear values—or, worse yet, meaningless ones—often leave individuals confused and therefore willing to compromise.

Without a clear and compelling vision and set of values, we founder, drifting far from our goals. We become easily influenced and distracted by outside forces. When employees fail to connect with vision and values, the result is a decline in morale and retention. Michael Useem, professor of management and director of the Center for Leadership and Change Management at the Wharton School, notes, "When I talk to very senior people at large companies, I consistently hear a statement that in their mind, the company vision and strategy are clear [to them], but people in the middle rank and on the front lines have not been able to fully appreciate that."[5]

The process of envisioning the future requires time, energy, and patience. It requires a strong sense of optimism and a belief what happens in the future is not the result of rolling the dice, but the consequence of conscious action. When leaders dismiss vision as frivolous or optional, it is only a matter of time before performance begins to decline. Many will testify that the decline of the American auto industry, leading insurance companies, and big investment houses, for example, was the result of a lack of vision—even as the world changed, these companies remained mired in their old ways of thinking. CEOs demanded performance without defining victory, required reports and financial analysis without galvanizing the hearts of their people. Vision and values are not merely statements to anchor an annual report; rather, they must be the source of inspiration that enables us to do the hard and right, as opposed to the easy and wrong.

A Picture Is Worth a Thousand Words

Leaders are often challenged to articulate a vision in a way that is inspiring and can be meaningfully communicated by others. For some, the process of formulating a vision is relatively easy; for others it is daunting. Yet without exception each of us, in our own way—implicitly or explicitly, verbally or pictorially, elaborately or simply —*can* create this idea of vision. Working with organizations or individuals, we have enabled people to envision by using the following strategies:

- Writing down sentences that articulate victory
- Closing our eyes and dreaming of what can be
- Drawing a picture with symbols enables us to capture the future
- Asking people to conduct a virtual walk in the future and have them capture the images they see
- Breaking down the vision into relevant components (for organizations, this could include client service, product development, operational procedure, or how people want to treat each other; for individuals, it could be holistic thinking about professional aspirations, personal desires, community responsibilities, and spiritual concerns)

> These exercises stimulate the creative side of the brain and serve as a memorable touch point for the team. Many executives have shared with us, years after they have done the exercise, that they still remember the process, words, pictures, and visions they created.

Inspiration is not enough. The famous statement of Thomas Edison applies: "Genius is 1 percent inspiration and 99 percent perspiration." In addition to a clear vision, then, we must have a plan to get us there.

FOCUSING ON RESULTS: FOLLOW A ROADMAP

A compelling vision and set of values encourages us to dream; a focused roadmap enables us to execute. Use of the term *execution* for this specific organizational context was popularized in 2002 by former Honeywell CEO Larry Bossidy and his co-author, leading executive coach Ram Charan, in their book *Execution*. In the book, the pair outlined the building blocks for achieving results. Their essential message was that in order to be effective at execution, leaders must be committed to people and processes. Leaders need an effective plan to anchor the dream in reality. The plan or approach must clearly outline the actions that people in the organization should take to achieve the desired results.

The problem most leaders face in outlining actions is not generating ideas or alternatives; rather, it is the difficulty of saying "no" to ideas and approaches that distract us from our focus. There is a dynamic tension in any organizational setting. On one side, leaders want to inspire their people to dream and contribute. On the other, leaders want to maintain the focus of the organization on the areas most critical for success. According to recent research released by Booz & Company, underperformance when it comes to actual results stems from a lack of focus. Based on a study of 1,800 global executives, 64 percent of senior managers report that they regularly have too many priorities, and 56 percent say that allocating resources in a way that really supports their strategy is a formidable challenge. According to the study, the key to success is choosing opportunities that suit the organization and learning to turn down many that, although they seem appealing on the surface, will only serve as a distraction. Maintaining focus often requires leaders to say "no." As one senior executive stated, "I get worn out saying *no*; I get tired of being the bad guy. Yet that is what is required to maintain the focus of the organization, especially during times of change."[6]

One way to help an organization maintain focus is by encouraging participation in the planning process. There are a variety of planning approaches, many with common elements such as developing a mission statement or statement of purpose, identifying key areas or critical success factors, conducting gap analysis, generating solutions, and action planning and follow-up. Each of these steps help organizations focus and marshal resources.

1. Develop a Mission Statement or Statement of Purpose

With the articulated vision as a guide, leaders need to extrapolate a more specific objective or goal. These aspirations have been called *mission statements, statements of purpose,* or *strategic intent* (a phrase popularized by Gary Hamel and C. K. Prahalad in their eponymous 1989 *Harvard Business Review* article).[7] An organization's strategic intent is a long-term goal that describes how it will live up to its vision. Strategic intent is generally succinct and focused, and it may provide a specific stretch target. For example: "Our coffee is in every supermarket in the Midwest."

Regardless of what you call it, a mission statement helps focus your actions and decisions. It explicitly expresses what you want to achieve and how you will measure success. In a sentence or two it defines *what we do, for whom, and for what purpose.* It also helps you prioritize your attention and focus your resources. Statements of purpose or mission statements run the gamut in terms of length and specificity. Compared to vision, defining the mission is more of a left-brain activity. Logic, analysis, and objectivity drive the process. Yet vision and its bookend—mission—are often confused. Vision inspires;

mission defines. Vision is what gets us up in the morning, whereas mission is what we do throughout the course of the day. Vision is held in our hearts and souls; mission is measured by clear standards and metrics. Vision indicates a sense of energy; mission enables progress toward a specific target. They are like the heart and the head—both critical elements of life and growth in any organization.

There is a tension in these types of statements between specificity and flexibility. For example, if your primary intent is to achieve an 18 percent return, then you are focused primarily on the numbers and the value chain. You can sell anything from microchips to hot dogs, as long as you hit the 18 percent return. But if instead your intent is to be the market leader in microchips, then you have to think about quality, design, and customers.

The more focused your intent, the less flexibility. Having a statement that is more specific or more flexible is not inherently right or wrong; rather, it requires thoughtful reflection and for the leader to be intentional. Johnson & Johnson, on the one hand, doesn't have a mission statement; instead, they have a one-page credo outlining their values as well as their responsibilities to customers, employees, the community, and stockholders. The Campbell Soup Company's mission statement, on the other hand, is short and simple: *Together we will build the world's most extraordinary food company.*

Regardless of length and specificity, a mission statement must stand the test of time and guide the actions of the entire cohort of employees. It requires a good deal of time and energy.

The more collaboration and participation in the creation of the statement, the more likely the sustainability and commitment from the organization.

2. Identify Three to Five Critical Success Factors

Once the mission has been clarified, the leader and the team need to identify three to five critical elements required for success. For instance, if the mission of an academic institution is to prepare future leaders, then they must identify the specific factors to focus on. Critical success factors (CSFs) in this case might include a relevant curriculum, qualified faculty, demanding workload, and community services.

The challenge for most leaders and organizations is not coming up with a list of key areas or CSFs; rather, it is narrowing the list to the most critical three to five. However, once a team has narrowed down the list and ranked their priority, decisions on budgeting, staffing, time allocation, and expending organizational energy become much easier.

3. Measure the Gaps

With the critical success factors in mind, the next step is to conduct a gap analysis.

A gap is no more than the distance between the desired state and the current condition for any key area. For example, if an organization's competitive advantage is people, then the desired state may be to have new staff trained in ninety days, with a retention rate of 75 percent. Currently, however, the time to train qualified staff may be 120 days and the retention rate 50 percent. The important goal of the gap analysis is to clarify the desired state. Often leaders identify priorities without ever defining what they mean. Gap analysis is an intentional step to start that discussion and clarify meaning. It requires us to take a realistic look at where we currently are—as ugly as that sometimes may be. If we are not willing to assess how bad or how wide the gap between our desired state and current state truly is, we have no hope of closing it.

Once the gaps have been clearly identified, we let the creative juices flow to explore solutions. This is another point where a leader can leverage the intellectual capital of the team through individual assignments or team exercises. The objective is to consolidate the creative power of the team and generate as many ideas as possible. The next task is to select the best solutions, because not all ideas are equal. Various techniques have been used for selecting, including 2x2 matrices and weighted criteria lists. Regardless of the specific techniques, it is essential that there be a rationale for the selection and that the implementing team understand what that rationale is. By understanding the rationale, the team will be more committed to the implementation and action plan.

4. Conduct Action Planning

Most leaders are familiar with some form of action planning. The specific format is less important than the fact that there is a clear roadmap of objectives and action steps. Objectives should be: specific, measurable, ambitious, relevant, and time-bound. Action steps should include the task to be accomplished, who is going to do it, and by when. A variety of software is available for formatting and tracking. The action plan enables the leader to delegate most of the activities. Thus it gives the leader the time and space needed to focus on strategy and the bigger picture.

5. Follow Up: Monitor Progress and Make Adjustments

This may seem like the most obvious step in any planning process, yet it is often the most overlooked. Leaders get distracted with other priorities, and the energy to create the plan begins to dissipate. How many of us attend multiple meetings that all seem the same? Like organizational *déjà vu*, we are discussing the same issues time and again. Why? We have failed to monitor and follow up on what we agreed to do in the previous planning meetings.

Measuring performance and evaluating progress requires a process that captures the data or results, yet does not overcomplicate matters. The setup depends on your intent or objective as well as the size of your organization. For our purposes here, it's not useful to delve into technical detail; however, it is useful to note that measurement requires a few basic elements.

First, you need to establish in advance what success looks like and what the performance measures are. They may be financial, such as a sales target, or they may be a ratio or percentage, such as your employee retention rate or same-store sales. In many cases an objective has more to do with something less tangible, such as brand, talent, and customer satisfaction. Regardless, there should be no mistaking your objective—you need to know what you are measuring.

Next, you need a framework to collect and organize the relevant information. If your target is sales-based, your own sales and past sales can be benchmarked against those of industry competitors. If your goal is more qualitative, then you might choose a scorecard as opposed to an established accounting method. You also need to determine how and how often the goal will be monitored and revisited. Tracking results may be an end to the planning process, but it should also provide a means for learning, and it can become the basis for future goals and aspirations.

The job of the leader is to ensure that results, accountability, and incentive are all coordinated in a way that suits the vision and organizational culture. The part of monitoring progress that is often neglected is communicating results to participants and stakeholders. Achieving results can empower an organization, just as missing the mark can cause a hit to morale. Remember to discuss outcome in total—accomplishments and contributions—and not just the quantitative output. As we've noted, most members of your organization will be at least as motivated to learn and demonstrate their competence by recognition of their contributions and opportunities as they will be by achieving financial goals.

PERSONAL COMMITMENT: REMAIN DEDICATED

As we have discussed previously, building a leadership pillar to achieve results requires more than a vision and a focused roadmap. The third requirement is the personal commitment and desire of the leader to succeed. This drive can be summarized in two words for the leader: *conviction* and *character*.

Conviction entails demonstrating, clearly and unequivocally, that the organization's objectives are ones that you personally believe in. To be the kind of leader that people respond to—someone who rises above the rest in terms of impact and accomplishments—you must have conviction, or "fire in the belly," to remain steadfast in the face of adversity. Conviction is the drive that motivates us to go forward despite immense emotional and logistical challenges.

Conviction is the passion that spurs us to make a difference. It is the laser focus on a higher purpose that differentiates a great leader from a merely competent one. Margaret Thatcher, for example, was determined to rescue Britain from economic demise when she introduced a market economy to the nation. She was a crusader who absorbed extreme criticism. To her supporters, Thatcher remains a transformative figure who saved Britain's economy, took the trade unions to task, and reestablished the nation as a world power. Jack Welch, another crusader for change, was obsessed with the idea that GE must hold the number one or number two spot in every business category—or else get out of it altogether. When Welch took control of the company, GE sales were just under $28 billion, with an estimated market value of around $14 billion. In the year he retired, GE was doing $130 billion in sales, with a value of $410 billion dollars. Closer to home, I am struck by the leadership of MIT's president, Susan Hockfield. In her own quiet and unassuming way, Hockfield is passionate about coaxing the academic institution into the twenty-first century. Driving change in an elite academic environment is not an easy task. Hockfield accomplishes it by building coalitions and bringing faculty and staff on board with her vision, one person at a time.

We have observed successful leaders from all walks of life and witnessed their relentless tenacity to achieve results and make a difference. This brand of conviction can be demonstrated in the drive to transform society, to mobilize organizations to improve performance, or to enrich communities. Fundamentally, conviction presents itself as a clear purpose that is rarely focused exclusively on making money. Financial benefits are a by-product of a leader's success in motivating others. As a driver of results, conviction is something that cuts across everything a leader does and decides.

After conviction, *character* is the second prerequisite for achieving results. It is necessary because it goes to the heart of why people follow your lead. Your character is the sum total of your words and your actions. People perceive it at every moment, and the effects are cumulative. Strong character is associated with certain behaviors, including perseverance. Perseverance enables a leader to remain committed to a plan when success does not happen quickly. If you have the perseverance to break through emotional and logistical barriers, then you bring others with you.

Another character attribute that drives results is *realistic optimism*. According to psychologist and author Martin E. Seligman, optimism allows us to see adversity as temporary. Doug Conant, former chief executive of the Campbell Soup Company, cites realistic optimism as one of the primary traits that helped him turn the company around during his ten-year tenure. Conant observed: "As a leader, my thinking always starts with the question: How can things be better? I find it much more interesting, and fruitful, to start with optimism and then to move quickly on how to execute against that aspiration."[8] Key among other traits of character that drive results are passion, flexibility, and integrity.

Passion enables a leader to keep moving forward in spite of tough times. Jeffrey Cohn, former executive at Spencer Stuart and author of the book *Why Are We Bad at Picking Good Leaders?*, points out that Jeff Bezos, the CEO of Amazon, "was ridiculed in 2001 for clinging to a company that many called 'Amazon.bomb.' " According to Cohn, it was Bezos's "inner passion that fueled his drive to keep pushing forward even in the darkest days of the dotcom crash, when the company was teetering on the brink of collapse."[9]

Integrity can be defined as the integration of inner values and outward actions. Leaders who "walk the talk" are able to motivate others because they lead by example. They demonstrate fortitude and honesty. Finally, flexibility—like agility—allows leaders to adapt their style and try something different when the current plan is not working. Like perseverance, flexibility helps you manage unexpected situations with effectiveness and dexterity.

PUTTING IT ALL TOGETHER: ADIDAS NORTH AMERICA

The athletic footwear industry in the United States has a major concentration of competitors in Portland, Oregon, and the close suburb of Beaverton. It is not uncommon to see executives in Portland and Beaverton moving from one footwear company to another. This is what happened, in the late 1980s, when Rob Strasser departed from Nike following a creative disagreement with founder Phil Knight. Without breaking stride, Strasser, along with long-time business partner Peter Moore, made his way over to Adidas. As it happened, this was a time in the industry's history known as "the sneaker wars," when Nike, Reebok, and Adidas were all vying for market share in the United States and Europe.

Strasser, a big bear of a man known for sporting Hawaiian shirts and a shaggy beard, had been Nike's dynamic marketing leader. It was he, along with Moore, who helped founder Phil Knight build the company into a thriving shoe and athletic apparel giant by introducing the Air Jordan shoe line, which featured basketball superstar Michael Jordan as sponsor.

It was a coup for Adidas to land Strasser, who became the CEO of the company's American business in 1993. His plan was to transform Adidas in the United States into the hip, high-performance brand for serious athletes, casting his former employer as the established, mass-market everyman's brand. In his six years at Adidas, Strasser's work helped elevate the company from eighth to third in the athletic footwear industry ranking in the United States. Tragically, the same year he made CEO, Strasser died suddenly of a heart attack at age forty-six, while attending the Adidas sales meeting in Munich, Germany. At the time, the company had only partially lived through its grand plan for brand transformation.

The person who, in 1995, was ultimately tapped to carry the torch at Adidas was Steven E. Wynne. At first glance, Wynne would have seemed an unlikely candidate to continue what marketing maverick Strasser had started. Prior to joining the company, Wynne was a partner in the law firm of Ater Wynne LLP and served as Adidas's outside counsel. He had never run a company before. But Wynne had a strong vision of what success could look like at Adidas and a plan for generating results.

When Steve Wynne became president and CEO of Adidas America, he was determined to live the dynamic dream, begun by Rob Strasser, of remaking Adidas as an elite, high-performance brand. He collaborated with the management team at Adidas to expand and define that vision in a way that could be disseminated throughout the organization. They talked about "celebrating the ideals of sport that are as present when a five-year-old kid steps up to a T-ball as they are when you play at the opening day game at Yankee Stadium."

Wynne's intent was as ambitious as it was specific. To the amazement of his board, his two-year goal was to grow Adidas from $400 million in revenue in North America to $1 billion—in just two years. At Adidas, where the product focus was more on function than fashion, Wynne organized teams to promote cooperation and creativity. The engagement norms between executives and employees were casual, titles were unimportant, and the dress code was informal.

Wynne's team examined their manufacturing and distribution organization first. The critical need to decrease end-to-end delivery from 180 days to three weeks surfaced a huge gap in their system. They determined that this particular gap was by far the most pressing. If they failed to address it, every other goal was irrelevant: the product would suffer, they would miss their financials, and people would lose their jobs. They went to work on closing the gap with an action plan. More important, they created a common focus on an immediate issue. At meetings, people consistently asked: *Does this [initiative] help us solve our distribution gap?* If not, it was put on hold.

A second CSF for the team was marketing. In an interview at the time, Wynne said, "We have taken on an independent sales agency group and turned it into a directly employed sales force. We've built an effective approach to dealing with key accounts, from a marketing standpoint and from a sales standpoint. We built an exceptional sales team in apparel, which has been consistent with the growth of that business. Basically, we have taken a real workmanlike view of building the fundamental operating parts of our business."

They also shifted gears to focus their marketing dollars in service of transforming the brand. Unable to match Nike on sponsorship dollar-for-dollar, Adidas put individual contracts aside and concentrated on exposure by signing exclusive contracts with a few of the sports world's most recognizable and successful franchises, such as the New Zealand All Blacks, the New York Yankees, and Notre Dame's Fighting Irish.

On February 19, 1997, the Portland *Oregonian* reported that Wynne had accomplished "one of the major marketing coups of its modern era." Adidas had beaten out Nike and Reebok to outfit the Notre Dame football team, announcing a five-year deal with Notre Dame that would see it provide footwear to the football team and footwear and apparel to "most" of the other twenty-six varsity sports. Wynne's laser focus had succeeded in catapulting his brand into the highest echelons of their target market.

Wynne also had the desire and conviction to succeed. When he joined Adidas it was a critical time for Adidas's aspirations to recover in the American market. They had lost their CEO very suddenly and tragically, in the midst of a critical change process. Their brand was in flux, and there was concern and unrest throughout the organization. Wynne rallied the management team, strengthened their commitment to the change, and kept most of the team intact and fully engaged. That stability and experience base allowed Wynne to continue the transformation without losing momentum.

In 1997, under Wynne's direction, Adidas achieved record results and passed the $1 billion mark in gross sales in the United States six months ahead of the plan. Today, Adidas AG is the largest sportswear manufacturer in Europe and the second biggest sportswear manufacturer in the world. A critical part of the brand's success was the turnaround in the United States, which was a product of Strasser's vision and Wynne's ability to extend that vision and manage for results.

LEADING FOR RESULTS

If we have learned anything from the recent "Great Recession," it is that leaders at public companies must be focused on much more than stock price. Although the goal of most is business growth, results transcend short-term financials.

Quarterly earnings are only a part of leading for the long term. Even Jack Welch, whose quest for competitive advantage was legendary and who is regarded as the father of "shareholder value," has said that focusing so heavily on quarterly profits and share price gains is a "dumb idea." The former GE chief told the *Financial Times* that the emphasis executives and investors place on shareholder value, which began gaining popularity after a speech he made in 1981, was misplaced.[10]

More recently, it has become abundantly clear that an important part of the leader's job is remaining in sync with the desires and values of the enterprise's customers. When customers wanted smaller, more fuel-efficient cars, beginning earlier in the decade, the auto industry was slow to respond, and it paid a steep price.

Leading with conviction means daring to think beyond the financials. We usually urge leaders to consider the future before they focus on the present. If you start designing your aspirations based on the current state, you needlessly constrain the future. By looking first at the future, you are inspired to think more broadly and boldly. Indeed, to survive and thrive in a continuously changing world, leaders must simultaneously focus on both the future and the day-to-day life of the organization and the individuals it comprises. And keep in mind that no strategy, even the most perfectly articulated, will succeed if the minds and hearts in the organization are not committed to it. Your job as a leader is to marshal those forces and keep them moving toward the goal.

Five Guiding Principles for Building a Pillar of Results:

1. Be clear on what you want to achieve, and relentlessly pursue it.
2. Chart out a roadmap that specifies the key areas that need to be addressed and the gaps that must be closed.
3. Establish a set of measurable objectives with supporting activities to realize the vision.
4. Unleash the power of your people to navigate the enterprise using a shared roadmap.
5. Measure progress constantly and consistently, reward model behaviors, and celebrate results.

10

The Journey Continues

Our habits are the product of our behaviors and our behaviors are the outcome of our values and values are our destiny.

—Mahatma Gandhi

The challenge of leading in today's environment of volatility is daunting. It is believed that fewer than 30 percent of all companies successfully implement their strategic plans.[1] Fewer than 50 percent of major restructuring projects at Fortune 1000 companies succeed.[2] Mergers and acquisitions are more likely to fail than to bear fruit—some estimate failure rates as high as 80 percent. The primary reason for the lack of success is not financial: it's leadership.[3]

According to the Center for Creative Leadership, leaders at all levels lack crucial skills that will enable them to succeed today and in the future, with only 30 percent perceived to be truly adept in collaboration and innovation.[4] That gap in style and skill has made it difficult to attract top talent; one survey shows that some 53 percent of organizations are now facing shortages in some areas.[5] Essentially, people want leaders who can articulate a compelling vision of the future and lead the way while allowing others to make unique contributions. We want our leaders to engage, challenge, and inspire us and help us to achieve more than we ever thought was possible. But how can leaders bridge the gap and grow? What path can they take to become better? What avenues are available to launch the leadership journey?

In its essence, leadership is, as Warren Bennis put it, a "process of becoming." We define *becoming* as an endless journey of overpowering our shortcomings. It is about changing the behaviors that constrain us and taking charge of our destiny. Like a sculptor contemplating a block of marble, we as leaders must create our own vision and determine how our actions will shape its contours and give it form and texture. We need to be aware of our capabilities and understand the terrain of the organization and the cultural landscape facing us. Only then, with persistence, passion, and sensitivity, can we begin to put chisel to stone.

Carl Jung believed that the *process of becoming* requires us to confront parts of ourselves that cause us pain and anger. We need to wrestle with the forces within us that hold us back, and we need to understand the origin of these forces as well as the impact they have on us. Ignoring the demons (such as ego and insecurity) that limit us is a recipe for repeated mistakes and serves to distance us from others. When we as leaders are ineffective or even abusive or demeaning, it is a result of a refusal to take a hard look in the mirror. That act of isolating ourselves from the truth about our shortcomings not only harms others but also causes inner pain for ourselves. Reflection, self-examination, meditation, and feedback are all elements that can help us deepen our understanding of ourselves and become better.

Self-reflection is the essence of our journey to lead with conviction. Before retiring to bed every night, for example, Winston Churchill reflected on the events of the day and asked himself: "What did I do well?" "What could I have done better?" "What behaviors do I need to work on for the future?" This simple and straightforward exercise is a starting point.

In launching our journey of becoming, we need to be aware of the many polarities we face both personally and professionally. Balancing work demands and personal needs, managing the technical aspects of our job while attending to people's concerns, designing a vision while focusing on operations, and stabilizing the enterprise while driving change are some of the polarities that we must consider. Moving between and among these opposing forces requires honesty and agility.

The process of becoming is a lifelong journey that entails persistence, patience, and practice. Likewise, embracing the nine pillars concept described in this book requires us to go slow before going fast. To walk before running. Therefore the best approach to the journey is to build and sustain one pillar at a time, line upon line, precept upon precept.

This book describes the skills, or pillars, that leaders need to build in order to lead with conviction, and it offers tools and advice to hone those particular skills. Yet starting the leadership journey also requires some specific *qualities.*

First and foremost, effective leaders are driven by an *energy that transcends material advancement.* Although accumulating wealth is a common aspiration, moving beyond material and physical rewards in order to satisfy our deeper desires offers a more powerful and sustainable motivation. For some, this deeper desire is to set a positive example for those around us. For others, it is to make a difference in people's lives and have a material impact on our world. Still others are deeply motivated by the positive legacy they will someday leave behind.

This brings to mind Sir Thomas Hunter, an entrepreneur and the first homegrown billionaire in Scotland. The son of a grocer, Hunter spent his childhood in the small village of Ayrshire, in a region of the country known for its coal. But when the coal industry in the region went into decline, it delivered a blow to the local economy. Business dried up, and Hunter's father was forced to close his grocery store. Legend has it that Hunter went to work selling sneakers out of the back of a van. The rest is history: Hunter went on to create Sports Division, one of the largest sporting goods chains in the UK.

After fourteen years he sold the business—cashing out. His intention at the time was to settle down with his family and live a life of means. But then Hunter stopped and took a look at his life, and something struck him. "I didn't want to be the richest man in the cemetery," he says.[6] That's when he started the Hunter Foundation to manage what he calls his venture philanthropy.[7] The foundation began by funding enterprise education in primary schools in Scotland and went on to team up with the Clinton Foundation to work on projects in Malawi and Rwanda. Hunter's commitment to helping others by sharing his wealth of knowledge and a spirit of winning despite all odds has increased his sense of purpose and happiness.

According to Jack McConnell, Scotland's former first minister: "[Hunter's] philanthropic work and the creative way that he has thrown himself into that has been one of the most significant drivers for change in Scotland in the last decade. The work his foundation does is all about being a catalyst for change, not a substitute and not a general giveaway but a genuine approach to change the way things are done."[8]

For leaders like Hunter, money is not the prime mover. He and others like him are motivated by compassion and a deep concern for helping others. They actualize their being by having a positive impact on society. In doing so, both they and society are transformed. In our work with students in universities throughout the world, we have met and been inspired by a number of individuals who are dedicated to the cause of making the world a better place. They are driven by a range of social causes, such as helping women in rural villages and becoming entrepreneurs in emerging economies, or providing educational opportunities for the less fortunate.

Above all, leadership is a calling to make a difference in the life of others. It compels us to transform countries, organizations, communities, and families as well as ourselves. This process is reciprocal. By contributing to others, leaders enrich others' lives and create meaning in their own. The desire to serve, to take initiative, to swim against the tide, to go beyond material and financial gains, is the most fundamental element of leadership.

A second marker that we have found along the journey to leading with conviction is *resilience*. Most effective leaders seem to be endowed with a will of steel. Despite failure, disappointment, and betrayal, they manage to bounce back with a renewed sense of purpose, a fighting spirit, and, in most cases, a deeper understanding. Most of them look at failure as boot camp, where the sweat and humiliation pay off by instilling in them a strong drive to start again with deeper humility and greater wisdom.

Resilience is the trait that sustains Li Qi, who rose through the ranks from bank cashier to chairwoman of the Bank of Deyang in China. Raised in a military family, she watched her father dedicate his entire life to his soldiers. Her father's example of total commitment inspired her. She went on to establish China's first Financial Service Center for Women. The primary mission for the Center was to provide female entrepreneurs with low-interest loans to start businesses throughout her province. In addition, she served as a party secretary and as deputy mayor in Luo Jiang. By 2010, the Bank of Deyang had reached total assets of $4 billion under Li Qi's leadership.

Yet the road was not easy for Li Qi on either a professional or a personal level. Making it as woman in a man's world was grueling. In banking, she had to overcome gender stereotypes, professional envy, and many obstacles thrown in her way. In her personal life she faced unbearable tragedies: losing her husband in a car accident and her only son to illness. Yet despite all this, she never complained or resorted to blame. And she never gave up on her vision to help women become successful business leaders. This kind of resilience is a fundamental element in sustaining the leadership journey. It allows us to face difficulties and hardships without backing down. More than that, it transforms hardship into a fuel that motivates us further.

The third quality that fortifies leadership conviction is a sense of *realistic optimism*. As effective leaders keep their "eyes on the prize," they do so with grace and lightness. They impose less and invite more. They encourage and empower others. There is a sense of positivity in their thinking and demeanor. They are propelled by the notion that tomorrow will be better. It is this positive mind-set that fuels their conviction.

This is the case for the legendary pediatric neurosurgeon Dr. Fred Epstein, who was the founding director of the Institute for Neurology and Neurosurgery (INN) at Beth Israel Hospital in New York City. Epstein had a tough childhood.

He was dyslexic and had difficulties keeping up in school. Over the years, Epstein lost interest altogether in his studies. But later, thanks to the efforts of one of his teachers and support from his aunt, Epstein overcame these challenges and started to excel. He studied at New York University, and after that he never looked back.[9]

Epstein's childhood experiences shaped his character as well as his mission in life. He understood what his young patients were going through, and he did everything in his power to create a positive environment while they were in his care. The INN was known for its upbeat atmosphere, with music, clowns, and fun activities developed by therapists.[10] "If you tell children that their future is limitless, and you give them enough love and encouragement, they'll believe you," Epstein once said. "And they'll believe in themselves. They'll form an inner vision of themselves that they can grow into."[11]

Despite his fame, Epstein remained humble and available. He listed his home phone number in the New York phone directory and welcomed calls from people who needed his help and guidance. The sign on his door read FRED. And Epstein's positive demeanor extended beyond his patients to colleagues. He established yoga sessions as a means of stress relief for staff members, for example.

Epstein's story reminds us that, among other things, by being positive and approachable we can have a broad impact. For example, research on positive thinking shows that being upbeat can be contagious.[12] Furthermore, experience tells us that a positive outlook engages people to come together and perform tasks with energy and creativity. We are also learning through research that positive thinking reduces stress and anxiety.[13] This evidence calls on leaders to maintain a positive outlook and be less driven by negative emotions. Leading with conviction requires setting a tone that inspires other people to bring their best efforts and ideas forward.

The fourth quality for leading with conviction is the *desire to learn and improve*—even if it means breaking away from your comfort zone. As we have described throughout this book, breaking through the barriers to personal growth is difficult but essential.

One case in point is the story of King George VI, whom many describe as a reluctant leader. George VI ascended to the throne in 1936, not because he was the heir but because his brother Edward VIII abdicated to marry the American socialite Wallis Simpson. The movie *The King's Speech* depicts his struggle to overcome a debilitating stammer and engage the people of Britain at a critical time in their history.

With World War II on the horizon, the king was expected to galvanize the country and lead the forces into war. Yet King George VI hardly seemed equipped for this mammoth task, and his people lacked confidence in his abilities. A leader, after all, also needed to act the part and exhibit authority. With the help of his wife and his speech therapist, Lionel Logue, the king eventually overcame his stammer, gained confidence, and found his voice, both literally as well as metaphorically. The transformation was nothing short of dramatic, and over time he was able to win the hearts of his people.

King George VI's story shows us that leadership skills can be learned and honed, if only we have the courage to make the attempt and persevere. The desire to learn and become better, to transcend our natural condition, in order to improve our lives and the lives of others, is the bedrock of great leadership. The willingness to change and learn is also what leads us to hold ourselves accountable for our mistakes. Through that humble accountability we can make improvements that eventually lead to breakthroughs in the journey of leading with conviction.

Taking our cues from mistakes and learning from adversity is the hallmark of inner strength. This was the case for a student of ours who was rejected by every medical school she applied to. Yet she never gave up on her dream of becoming a physician. She was accepted to an Italian medical school and learned Italian before she began her studies. This was the case for a supervisor we worked with who was fired for no obvious cause, who instead of getting angry went on to explore new and better opportunities. Failing and moving on is the secret to renewal. The great leaders among us learn from the past. They use it as a mirror to understand themselves, their vulnerabilities, their mistakes, and their egos. And from that they rebound to make a difference in the lives of others.

All of these qualities, and the skills described throughout this book, reinforce our ability to lead with conviction. Conviction, after all, is the fuel that feeds the fire; it drives our actions; it is a compass pointing north.

In sum, searching for oneself and being willing to recognize strengths and weaknesses is crucial. Striking a balance between tasks and people and committing to change, through mentoring and coaching, are essential. Building a safe environment for people to venture and to be creative, as well as addressing conflicts constructively, through genuine compassion and collaboration, are paramount for leading with conviction. Finally, a leader's agility and ability to bring people together, by understanding their needs and inspiring them with a compelling vision and a challenging roadmap, can enable others to deliver meaningful results, fulfill their promise, and live out their promise, hopes, and dreams.

Notes

Introduction

1. Abraham Zaleznik, *The Managerial Mystique: Restoring Leader-ship in Business* (New York: Harper & Row, 1989), 116.
2. James Canton, *The Extreme Future* (New York: Dutton, 2006), 3–22.
3. Kerry Bunker and Michael Wakefield, "In Search of Authentic-ity—Now More Than Ever, Soft Skills Are Needed," *Leadership in Action* 24, no. 1 (March-April 2004): 16.
4. Ibid.
5. Robert Safian, "This Is Generation Flux: Meet the Pioneers of the New (and Chaotic) Frontier of Business," *FastCompany.com*, January 9, 2012.
6. Neelima Mahajan and Indrajit Gupta, "Mintzberg Unplugged," *Businessworld*, September 27, 2004.

Chapter One: The Pillar of Self

1. Warren G. Bennis and Burt Nanus, *Leaders: Strategies for Taking Charge* (New York: Harper & Row: 1985.)
2. Glenn Rifkin, "How Richard Branson Works Magic," *Strategy+Business*, October 1, 1998.

3. Lucy Kellaway, "Business Leaders Are Worse Than They Think," *Financial Times*, March 13, 2011.

4. Bill George, *True North* (San Francisco: Jossey-Bass, 2007), xxiii.

5. From the *Tao Te Ching*, a classic Chinese text. Although the text's authorship and date of compilation are still debated, according to tradition it was written around the sixth century B.C. by the sage Laozi, a record-keeper at the Zhou Dynasty court.

6. Warren G. Bennis and Robert J. Thomas, "Crucibles of Leadership," *Harvard Business Review*, September 2002.

7. Joseph Luft, *Of Human Interaction* (Mountain View, CA: Mayfield, 1959), 5.

8. Isabel Briggs with Peter B. Myers, *Gifts Differing: Understanding Personality Type* (Mountain View, CA: Davies-Black Publishing, 1980, 1995).

Chapter Two: The Pillar of Balance

1. Marcella Bombardieri, "Summers' Remarks on Women Draw Fire," *Boston Globe*, January 17, 2005.

2. Ronald A. Heifetz and Marty Linsky, *Leadership on the Line: Staying Alive Through the Dangers of Leading* (Boston: HBR Press, 2002), 252.

3. Cary Cherniss, "What Is Emotional Intelligence and Why It Matters," *Consortium for Research on Emotional Intelligence in Organizations*, paper presented at the Annual Meeting of the Society for Industrial and Organizational Psychology, New Orleans, LA, April 15, 2000.

4. Gregory J. Feist, *The Psychology of Science and the Origins of the Creative Mind* (New Haven, CT: Yale University Press, 2006), 151.

5. W. Chen and R. Jacobs, *Competence Study* (Boston, MA: Hay/McBer, 1997).

6. Chi-Sum Wong and Kenneth S. Law, "The Effects of Leader and Follower Emotional Intelligence on Performance and Attitude: An Exploratory Study," *Leadership Quarterly* 13, no. 3, *Elsevier Science* (June 2002), 243–274.

7. Melissa Kirn and Joe Light, "On the Lesson Plan: Feelings: 'Soft Skills' Business Courses Aim to Prepare Students for Management Roles," *Wall Street Journal*, July 7, 2011.

8. Roger Martin, *The Opposable Mind: Winning Through Integrative Thinking* (Boston: HBR Press, 2002).

9. Warren Bennis and Robert Townsend, *Reinventing Leadership* (New York: William Morrow, 1995), 7.

10. David P. Rakel, Theresa J. Hoeft, et al., "Practitioner Empathy and the Duration of the Common Cold," *Family Medicine*, July-August 2009, 494–500.

Chapter Three: The Pillar of Agility

1. The situational leadership theory was developed by Paul Hersey, professor and author of the book *Situational Leader*, and Ken Blanchard, leadership guru and author of *The One Minute Manager*, while working on the first edition of *Management of Organizational Behavior* (now in its 9th edition). For more, see http://www.amazon.com/Situational-Leader-Dr-Paul-Hersey/dp/0446513423 and http://en.wikipedia.org/wiki/The_One_Minute_Manager.

2. W. Chan Kim and Renee Mauborgne, "Parables of Leadership," *Harvard Business Review*, July-August 1992, 124.

Chapter Four: The Pillar of Change

1. Warren E. Buffett, *Letter to the Shareholders of Berkshire Hathaway Inc.* (March 1, 1999), 9. http://www.berkshirehathaway.com/letters/1998pdf.pdf.

2. Arthur Yeung, Ward Niou, and Nancy Dai, "Mary Kay China: Enriching Women's Lives," *China Europe International Business School*, 1–3. http://www.ft.com/intl/cms/2e7503b0 -74a7-11db-bc76-0000779e2340.pdf.

3. David Barboza, "Direct Selling Flourishes in China," *New York Times*, December 15, 2009.

Chapter Five: The Pillar of Conflict

1. This example is a composite based on two separate companies. The names and dates have been changed.

2. Jeff Weiss and Jonathan Hughes, "Want Collaboration? Accept—and Actively Manage—Conflict," *Harvard Business Review*, March 2005.

3. Scott Kirsner, "These Executives Love Risk," *Fast Company*, December 31, 1998.

4. M. Deutsch and P. Coleman (Eds.), *The Handbook of Conflict Resolution: Theory and Practice* (San Francisco: Jossey-Bass, 2000).

5. Figure 5.1: from "Conflict and Negotiation Process in Organizations" by K. Thomas, 1992. In M. D. Dunnette and L. M. Hough (Eds.), *Handbook of Industrial and Organizational Psychology* (2nd ed., vol. 3, p. 660). Palo Alto, CA: Consulting Psychologists Press. Copyright 1992 by L. M. Hough. Adapted by permission.

6. Table 5.1: Adapted by permission from "Conflict and Negotiation Process in Organizations" by K. Thomas, 1992. In M. D. Dunnette and L. M. Hough (Eds.), *Handbook of Industrial and Organizational Psychology* (2nd ed., vol. 3, p. 660). Palo Alto, CA: Consulting Psychologists Press. Copyright 1992 by L. M. Hough.

7. Mark Gerzon, *Leading Through Conflict: How Successful Leaders Transform Differences into Opportunities* (Boston, MA: Harvard Business Review Press, 2006).

Chapter Six: The Pillar of Creativity

1. From a restaurant review on Tripadvisor.com.

2. "Ferran Adrià and El Bulli—Risk, Freedom and Creativity," brochure published by Government of Catalonia, Presidential Department, Directorate General of Citizen Attention and Communication.

3. Ibid.

4. Katy McLaughlin, "Portrait of the Artist as a Chef," *Wall Street Journal*, October 31, 2008.

5. "Fast Times with Ferran Adrià," *Food & Wine*, February 2005.

6. John Carlin, "If the World's Greatest Chef Cooked for a Living, He'd Starve," *Guardian*, December 11, 2006.

7. "Ferran Adrià at Google," blogpost on http://atozin.blogspot.hk/2008/10/ferran-adri-google.html.

8. "Connecting Innovation to Profit: Five Key Insights from the World's Leading Entrepreneurs," Ernst & Young, 2010.

9. Teresa Amabile, "The Three Threats to Creativity," *HBR blog*, November 15, 2010. http://blogs.hbr.org/hbsfaculty/2010/11/the-three-threats-to-creativit.html.

10. Jim Andrew, Joe Manget, David C. Michael, Andrew Taylor, and Hadi Zablit, "Innovation 2010: A Return to Prominence—and the Emergence of a New World Order," BCG Perspectives, April 16, 2010.

11. Ibid.

12. Gregory Berns, *Iconoclast: A Neuroscientist Reveals How to Think Differently* (Boston: Harvard Business Review Press, 2008).

13. Robert Epstein, "Capturing Creativity," *Psychology Today* (July-August 1996).

14. Amy Novotney, "The Science of Creativity," *GradPSYCH*, American Psychological Association (January 2009).

15. Frans Johansson, *The Medici Effect* (Boston: Harvard Business School Publishing, 2006).

16. Lynda Gratton, *Hot Spots: Why Some Teams, Workplaces, and Organizations Buzz with Energy—and Others Don't* (San Francisco: Berrett-Koehler, 2007).

17. Berns, *Iconoclast*, 7.

18. Ibid.

19. Martin, "How Successful Leaders Think" (ch. 2, n. 10).

20. See Jerry Rhodes's work on Effective Intelligence at http://www.effectiveintelligence.com/home.aspx.

Chapter Seven: The Pillar of Coaching

1. J. McGovern, M. Lindemann, M. Vergara, S. Murphy, L. Barker, and R. Warrenfeltz, "Maximizing the Impact of Executive Coaching: Behavioral Change, Organizational Outcomes, and Return on Investment," *Manchester Review* 6, no. 1 (2001).

2. "Study: Student Coaching Increases Retention, Graduation Rates," *Huffington Post*, November 3, 2011.

3. Neelima Mahajan, "The Danger of Broken Leadership Pipelines," interview with Noel Tichy, *Times of India*, August 8, 2006.

4. Diane Coutu and Carol Kauffman, "What Can Coaches Do for You?" *Harvard Business Review*, January 2009.

5. Robert K. Greenleaf (author), Larry C. Spears (author, editor), and Stephen R. Covey (foreword), *Servant Leadership: A Journey into the Nature of Legitimate Power and Greatness*, 25th anniversary ed. (Mahwah: Paulist Press, 2002).

6. Derek Lehmberg, Glenn Rowe, John R. Philips, and Roderick E. White, "General Electric: An Outlier in CEO Talent," *Ivey Business Journal*, January-February 2009.

7. Adapted from Chen Kuan-Chung, "The Legend Basketball Coach John Wooden—a Case Study in Leadership," United

States Sports Academy, *The Sport Digest*—ISSN: 1558–6448, 2002–2010.

8. John Wooden and Jack Tobin, *They Call Me Coach* (New York: Tata McGraw-Hill, 2003).

9. Frank Litsky and John Branch, "John Wooden, Who Built Incomparable Dynasty at U.C.L.A., Dies at 99," *New York Times*, June 4, 2010.

Chapter Eight: The Pillar of Collaboration

1. Kenneth E. Smith and Debra A. Adams, "With St. Regis Merger Complete, Champion to Be Top Producer," *Pulp & Paper*, November 1985, 113.

2. Liz Wiseman and Greg McKeown, *Multipliers: How the Best Leaders Make Everyone Smarter* (New York: HarperBusiness, 2010).

3. J. Richard Hackman, *Leading Teams: Setting the Stage for Great Performances* (Boston: Harvard Business Review Press, 2002).

4. Jon R. Katzenbach & Douglas K. Smith, *The Wisdom of Teams: Creating the High-Performance Organization* (Boston: Harvard Business School Press, 1993).

5. Morten Hansen, *Collaboration: How Leaders Avoid the Traps, Create Unity, and Reap Big Results* (Boston: Harvard Business School Press, 2009).

6. Scott E. Page, *The Difference: How the Power of Diversity Creates Better Groups, Firms, Schools, and Societies* (Princeton: Princeton University Press, 2007).

7. IBM Global CEO Study 2006, March 2006.

8. Jon R. Katzenbach, "The Myth of the Top Management Team," *Harvard Business Review*, November 1997.

9. Douglas R. Conant, "Building Effective Teams Isn't Rocket Science, But It's Just as Hard," *HBR Blog Network*, April 4, 2012. http://blogs.hbr.org/cs/2012/04/consistently_building _highly_e.html.

Chapter Nine: The Pillar of Results

1. Steve Hamm and Geri Smith, "One Laptop Meets Big Business," *BusinessWeek*, June 5, 2008.

2. James Urquhart, "Digital Visionary: Nicholas Negroponte," *BBC News*, November 28, 2007.

3. Jean Noel Kapferer, *The New Strategic Brand Management*, 5th ed. (London: Kogan Page, 2012), 55.

4. Bill George and Peter Sims, *True North: Discover Your Authentic Leadership* (San Francisco: Jossey Bass, 2007).

5. Neelima Mahajan, interview with Michael Useem on his book *The Leader's Checklist: 15 Mission-Critical Principles* (Philadelphia: Wharton Digital Press, 2011).

6. "Executives Say They're Pulled in Too Many Directions and That Their Company's Capabilities Don't Support Their Strategy," Booz & Company, January 18, 2011. http://www.booz .com/global/home/press/article/49007867.

7. Gary Hamel and C. K. Prahalad, "Strategic Intent," *Harvard Business Review* (May-June 1989), 63–76.

8. Douglas R. Conant, "The Power of Idealistic-Realism: How Great Leaders Inspire and Transform," *HBR Blog Network*, January 12, 2012. http://blogs.hbr.org/cs/2012/01/the_power _of_idealistic-realis.html.

9. Jeffrey Cohn and Jay Moran, *Why Are We Bad at Picking Good Leaders? A Better Way to Evaluate Leadership Potential* (San Francisco: Jossey Bass, 2011).

10. Francesco Guerrera, "Welch Condemns Share Price Focus," *Financial Times*, March 12, 2009.

Chapter Ten: The Journey Continues

1. Jason D. Schloetzer, Matteo Tonello, and Melissa Aguilar, CEO Succession Practices 2012, *The Conference Board*, April 2012, R-1492-12-RR.
2. Wharton Executive Education, "*Leading Organizational Change.*" http://executiveeducation.wharton.upenn.edu/open -enrollment/leadership-development-programs/leading -organizational-change-program.cfm.
3. Matthias M. Bekier, Anna J. Bogardus, and Tim Old, "Why Mergers Fail," *McKinsey Quarterly*, no. 4 (2001).
4. Andre Martin, "What's Next? A CCL Research White Paper: The 2007 Changing Nature of Leadership Survey," Center for Creative Leadership, 2007.
5. ManpowerGroup, 2012 *Talent Shortage Survey*. http://www .manpowergroup.us/campaigns/talent-shortage-2012/.
6. Sir Thomas Hunter said this at a talk at Cheung Kong Graduate School of Business, Beijing, on April 24, 2012.
7. Kirsty Scott, "In the Last Decade His Philanthropic Work Has Been One of the Most Significant Drivers for Change in Scot- land," *Guardian*, January 1, 2009. http://www.guardian.co.uk /theguardian/2009/jan/02/sir-tom-hunter-profile.
8. Ibid.
9. Fred J. Epstein, M.D., "What'll Become of Fred?" *Reader's Digest*, February 1994.
10. From the website of Making Headway Foundation, http://www .makingheadway.org/who_we_are.php.

11. "The Doctor with Dyslexia," *Bright Star*, July 17, 2011, http://
    community.brightstar-learning.com/2011/thedoctorwithdy
    slexia/.
12. Melissa Dahl, "Your Happiness Could Be Contagious,"
    NBCNews.com, April 12, 2008.
13. Felicia A. Huppert, "Psychological Wellbeing: Evidence Regard-
    ing Its Causes and Consequences," *UK Government's Foresight
    Project, Mental Capital and Wellbeing*, September 2008.

About the Authors

Shalom Saada Saar is cofounder of the Center for Leadership Development. He teaches at Cheung Kong Graduate School of Business and at MIT. His work focuses on enhancing leadership effectiveness through self-awareness and organizational change. Shalom has consulted numerous organizations and coached senior executives throughout the world. He taught at Harvard University, SMU, China Europe International Business School in Shanghai; and he has delivered speeches on the power of leadership in mobilizing people and organizations. Shalom received his bachelor in economics and psychology from Swarthmore College and master and doctoral degrees in organizational behavior from Harvard University.

Michael J. Hargrove is cofounder of the Center for Leadership Development. He has led large-scale change efforts for global companies. His work has focused on improving performance by leveraging strategic thinking with collaborative leadership. He received his master and doctoral degrees in planning and organizational behavior from Harvard University.

Index

Soft thinking styles, 126, 127, 128, 129

South African rugby team, 46

Spain, restaurant innovation in, 113–116

Specificity, in mission statement, 196

Spencer Stuart, 203

Sponsorship, 207

Spontaneity, orientation of, 18

Sports Division, 214–215

Springboks, 46

Stability, balancing change and, 36–37

Stakeholder engagement, in change management, 87

Stanford University, 135

Starbucks, 189

Start-ups, 36–37

Statement of purpose, 195–197

Stating, as leadership tool, 54

Status quo, 21, 76, 79, 91, 150

Storming stage, 181, 182

Strasser, R., 204–205, 208

Strategy+Business, 3–4

Strengths: self-awareness of, 8, 221; team role definition based on, 179

Structural change, 84

Structure: individual orientation of, 18; team, 179–181

Subjectivity: balance between objectivity and, 35; "soft color" thinking styles with, 126, 127, 128, 129

Summers, R., 23–24, 25, 26, 37

Sun Tzu, 10, 44, 45

Supportive, being: in change management, 78; leadership tool of, 58–60. *See also* Coaching

Surgeons, 35, 47–48, 217–218

Synergy, 132

Systems, disruption of, 79–80, 84

T

T'ai (Prince), 59–60

Talent war, xxvii–xxviii

Tan, C.-M., 2

Tao Te Ching, 224n. 5

Taoism, 10–12

Taxonomy of Learning Domains, 124

Teaching, as leadership tool, 54. *See also* Coaching

Team Scorecard, 182–183

Teams: benefits of collaboration and, 167–169; collaboration and, 161–185; communication within, 179–181; complexity and, 161–163, 164, 165–167; conflict in, 91, 173–174; cultural differences and, 166–167; diversity in, 131–132, 166–167, 175; dysfunctions of, 172–174, 180–181; efficiency of, 169–170; functions of, 172–174; fundamentals of, 174–184; guiding principles for, 184–185; impact of high-functioning, 163; leadership and oversight of, 181–184; lifecycle stages of, 181–182; organizational environment for, 163; participation of, in goal setting, 177–178;